THE ISLAND INGREDIEN'

TOBY TOBIN-DOUGAN was born in Coventry, and in 1976 won a place at Hornsey College of Art in north London, where he gained an honours degree in photography. He later opened his own developing and printing laboratory and worked with the country's most renowned fashion, advertising and editorial photographers.

His first visit to St Martin's, Isles of Scilly, in 1982 was the start of a lasting love affair with the islands and the origin of an undiminishing desire to capture their wild beauty with his camera, as this volume shows. Teaching himself to bake out of sheer necessity, he converted a redundant barn into St Martin's Bakery and went on to gain the accolade of Best UK Food Retailer from Radio 4's Food Programme in 2002. In partnership with his former wife Elizabeth McPherson, he purchased the island public house, *The Seven Stones*, early in 2007. With the help of their children Darcy and Sean and of the other staff members, and through the inspired recruitment of a young and talented chef, Paul Websdale, they have transformed the business into a place of great success.

PAUL WEBSDALE was born in 1984 and achieved his cookery degree in 2002. He first came to the Scillies in 1996 and returned to the islands in 2002 as commis chef at the Hotel on St Martin's. After working for Michael Caines and for Martin Burge, he returned to St Martin's Hotel in 2004 as chef de partie. In 2007 he began his third spell on St Martin's, with his own kitchen at *The Seven Stones*. He likes to spend the winters travelling and learning as he works his way around the world.

This is the story of their journey and their aspirations.

Contact The Bakery, Higher Town, St Martin's on 01720 423444
or The Seven Stones, Lower Town on 01720 423560
www.theislandingredient.co.uk

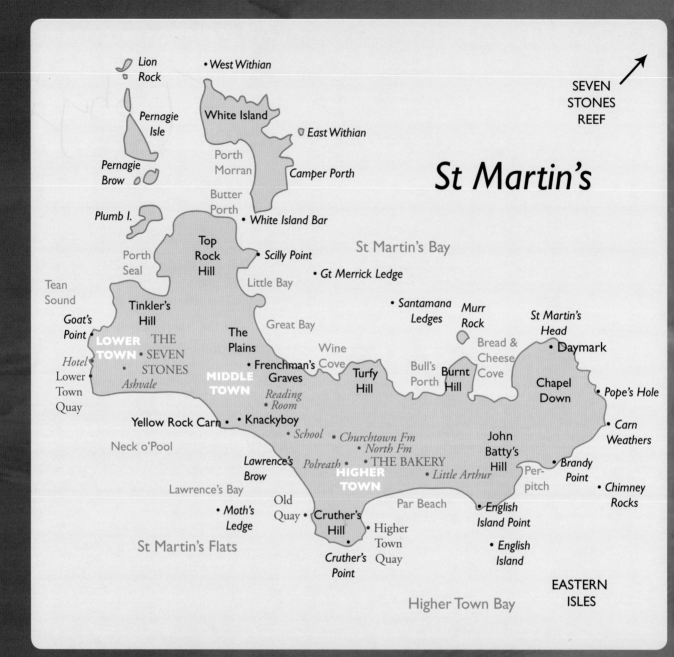

St Martin's

SEVEN STONES REEF

Lion Rock
West Withian
Pernagie Isle
White Island
East Withian
Porth Morran
Camper Porth
Pernagie Brow
Butter Porth
Plumb I.
White Island Bar
Top Rock Hill
Porth Seal
Scilly Point
St Martin's Bay
Little Bay
Gt Merrick Ledge
Tean Sound
Tinkler's Hill
Great Bay
Santamana Ledges
Murr Rock
St Martin's Head
Goat's Point
LOWER TOWN
THE SEVEN STONES
The Plains
Wine Cove
Bread & Cheese Cove
Daymark
Hotel
Frenchman's Graves
Turfy Hill
Bull's Porth
Burnt Hill
Chapel Down
Lower Town Quay
MIDDLE TOWN
Ashvale
Reading Room
Pope's Hole
Yellow Rock Carn
Knackyboy
School
Churchtown Fm
Carn Weathers
Neck o'Pool
North Fm
John Batty's Hill
Brandy Point
Lawrence's Brow
Polreath
THE BAKERY
HIGHER TOWN
Little Arthur
Per-pitch
Chimney Rocks
Lawrence's Bay
Old Quay
Par Beach
English Island Point
Moth's Ledge
Cruther's Hill
Higher Town Quay
English Island
St Martin's Flats
Cruther's Point
Higher Town Bay
EASTERN ISLES

St Martin's is the north-easterly island of Scilly, facing Land's End, which is twenty-eight miles away and to be seen on a clear day from Daymark, the seventeenth-century navigational aid which dominates one end of the island. Seven miles from Daymark to the north-east lies the Seven Stones reef, guarded by its lightship, while a mile and a quarter west of White Island, the beam of Round Island light sweeps over St Martin's. The powerful lamp on Bishop Rock, to the south-west and considerably further away, also lights up the night sky. A good night reveals five more lighthouse beams in all, surrounding the Cornish mainland. The loom of Île Vierge lighthouse on the north coast of France, ninety-six miles away, can also be seen on some nights on the undersides of clouds, to the south-east.

THE ISLAND INGREDIENT

TOBY TOBIN-DOUGAN
PAUL WEBSDALE

FOREWORD BY JUDE LAW

GREY MULLET PUBLISHING
SCILLY

First published March 2008
by Grey Mullet Publishing
Ganilly, Higher Town, St Martin's, Isles of Scilly TR25 0QL
Design and editorial services by Colum Hayward Consultancy
(colum@polairpublishing.co.uk)

Text © Copyright, Toby Tobin-Dougan and Paul Websdale, 2008
All photographs © Toby Tobin-Dougan, 2008 except: photograph p. 11 © Rob Young 2008;
p. 31, © Sandra Gibson; p. 66, from the Richards Collection, reproduced courtesy of the Morrab
Library, Penzance; p. 132, and main front cover photo, © Amaranthe Frost 2008

British Library Cataloguing-in-Publication Data
A catalogue record for this book is available from the British Library

ISBN 978-0-9558353-0-8

ACKNOWLEDGMENTS
*The businesses, Bakery and Seven Stones alike, would be nowhere without
their wonderful suppliers who are, in our view, the best in the world.
Sources here on Scilly have been most generous and forthcoming with their stories and memories
and the vital information they have given to enable this book to come to fruition. Toby in particular is eternally
grateful to those who were patient enough to be photographed. He writes, 'I should like particularly to thank Keith
Low for sharing his intimate wisdom and knowledge of the changes that he has seen take place within his lifetime;
and John (JJ) Goddard for his stories of the building of the Seven Stones and the Torrey Canyon disaster of 1967.
My special thanks go to Colin Daly, who provided detailed insight into the vital introduction of kelp burning to the
Island. Colin also illuminated the important part the wreck of the Association on Scilly played in the history of
navigation; he also told the story of the introduction of mains electricity to St Martin's in 1986. Thanks also to
St Martin's diver, Tim Allsop, who has supplied navigational information, enabling our records to be accurate.
Henrietta Graham, a renowned artist, did me the honour of asking me to sit for the portrait on page 189.'
This book would not have been possible without the foresight, encouragement, hard work and creative
design of Colum Hayward, and also the tireless and patient proofreading of Juliet Hemming.
Not forgotten: grateful thanks to Carla Roma.*

Printed in Great Britain by
Croxsons Ltd, Chesham, Bucks.

CONTENTS

SALAD DRESSINGS, SAUCES, OILS AND INGREDIENTS · 99

PASTIES, PIES AND PIZZAS · 109

FOREWORD

Few places in the world are as private or hold such
personal affection as St Martin's does for me. It reminds me
of all the good things, not only about England, but the world on
which we live: a beautiful environment filled with changing skies,
empty beaches, soaring rocks and rolling green. Peaceful people
living at life's sensible pace and a community with enough
sense of self to embrace visitors warmly. My family never
feel safer than there; I never feel happier.

JUDE LAW

It wasn't a sunrise to rush toward with the camera, or for lovers to point at

with an amazed finger. Even the birds were quiet in anticipation. An unusual calm and serenity prevailed after the passions of the wild winter weather, with the Eastern Isles occasionally appearing like a silk-screen vision and the sea an abandoned pane of glass. The sun struggled to lift itself under the heavy weight of the silver moisture that kept it clinging to the horizon. Nothing stirred, and an expectant beach lay as strips of contrasting story: dunes of undulating, eye-closing whiteness, sharply cut by the glistening compactness of the smoothing, receding tide.

Swarming sanderlings, at last disturbed by our intrusion, reluctantly settled again along by the standing stones as the dogs reared in mock confrontation, like two silhouetted dragons against a sun-shattered shore. Vacated crab-shells of olive, gold and blue lay upturned between the single strands of determined grasses that rested inside the circle of delineation they had etched in windier times. The gaining sun threw footsteps into bursts of radiating liquid as we walked the length of the beach.

Stopping on English Island Point, I was struck by the total lack of colour on this usually pigment-saturated landscape. Interpenetrating panes of silver mist cloaked Higher Town Quay and hinted now and then at where St Mary's once had stood.

And no birds sang.

The exhilarating shiver that brushed my neck was not of cold, nor was it sadness, for this fleeting glimpse of awareness had the emotion of a first kiss. We three stood. To lift the camera would have given a picture that was one-dimensional. I looked, and then turning for home felt the warmth of the winning sun on my left cheek, saw the two dogs in ecstatic chase of some unseen animal, and felt the stones colliding in my shabby pocket.

This fleeting picture, twenty-two years after my first fall onto St Martin's, had evaporated within seconds. The breeze shook the dew from the persistent marram grass, the birds awoke, and our footsteps like all those before were reclaimed by greedy waves.

CHAPTER 1: ARRIVAL

I *arrived in love and then fell once again, as many* do. Stepping onto Higher Town Quay the first time in 1982 was the start of a long love affair: senses rendered senseless, ears battered by boat, tractor and the sea, eyes surrounded by the sea and compressed by the sky.

The scene was then as it is now: men with rough chamois-toned skin and toothless smiles, leaning against rust-coloured vehicles teetering on a patchwork of cracked concrete. The sea was so clear that to step onto it felt possible. Our London luggage was tractor-buried by other similar baggage and then mounted and

Arum lilies and whistling jacks

squatted on by our fellow travellers. I felt naked, removed and excited by our short journey.

Flowers that I had never really looked at. Butterflies that I had never caught. The small strips of fields reaching for the sky. The drowning sound of our tractor. Nobody spoke. Bleached gates filled the gaps of jigsaw-laid granite walls that partly obscured distant wildernesses, and the shell-shining road weaved its narrow way along the spine of the island.

Our civilised tent was erected on rough grass, and the items of normality arranged in some semblance of order. Meanwhile the sun popped the seeds from the nearby-parched gorse pods, while the brave thrush plundered the contents of our canvas home and with tilted head planned her next attack.

The darkness and silence of that first night was only broken by the rustling of some small animal and by my own breathing. My worried investigation, with chilled bare feet on dew-drenched grass, was soon forgotten as, neck tipped back, I reeled at the sight of overhead stars. From horizon to horizon every inch was filled with a glittering fullness. My first shooting star, streaking like a spent firework, disappeared before I could focus, and a single ghostly cloud moved silently and relentlessly along. I was dwarfed by the sky and had become a mere fragment in this vast landscape.

*

THE NEXT two weeks blurred between days of beach-sweltering dizziness, shaken alive again by the numbing cold of the cruelly inviting sea. Impervious bracken bordered the labyrinth of footpaths that led us I knew not where, but ended in panoramic scenes of spectacular breathlessness. During our languid wanderings, the overpowering coconut aroma of gorse combined with the trodden wild garlic to assault the nose; while the fields of foxgloves, like standing crowds, sent me into a photographic frenzy.

On the shore, the gulls circled low and angrily above our heads as we cliff-scrambled, prising shards of long-lost pottery from wind and wave-weathered faces of rock. This now empty beach would one day see the arrival of our daughter and son. They would sit inside rings of shells, naked but for their white hats and sand-covered legs.

In the evenings, the phosphorescence of the foot stirred the shore. Mass invasions by feverish civilisations of dancing sandhoppers wondered and terrified me while, as ever, gently and quietly, the oval red sun fell behind the mechanised shine of Round Island light. Inevitably the quivering chill of night arrived, and once again the slow dying of campfires allowed the rapid arrival of total darkness. I closed my eyes; I can't remember sleeping.

*

THE RETURN home to London after those two weeks was brutal, an awakening, after the light of St Martin's: the dark Soho basement of my photographic business. In a lonely penance, I began to recall the visions I had witnessed, and slowly the growing ache began. Many more visits followed, each and every drawn-out year, as the faces and the landscape grew familiar. Departure from the island became a wrench that worsened each year, and the normality of work, commute and mortgage grew to be abnormality in comparison with the freedom of the giant skies and the bewitching landscape of St Martin's.

The seed of mutiny had been sown in me and grew steadily. I was coming to a decision, and I began to dream of the dream.

*

THERE WERE to be another ten years of blissful holidaying and agonised waiting before I forever turned my back on the mainland, to begin this story of discovery and to try and live the dream. I was not the first. Here on the island we are all,

Oystercatchers, winter morning

more or less, escapees: none more so than those who have chosen to run away to reality.

I shall never forget the feeling of separation, isolation and trepidation with which I arrived. The turning of the back and the burning of bridges was to hit me like a wave. I had left children, wife, friends, family and business behind, and the decision was absolute and irreversible. A terrible sickness invaded my body, while my mind was a frenzy of regret and doubt.

Nor shall I ever forget the kindness of Keith the fisherman, who collected a sad, forlorn and frightened person from Lower Town Quay those many years ago, and who would not only share his house and table but would also teach me the ways of the island. We collected firewood from the abandoned hedges to warm his spartan house. He would show me the wonders of shooting nets for elusive grey mullet by moonlight, teach me how to pull gaff-nosed conger eels from dank smelling chasms at the extremes of tides, and show me where the unseen woodcock lay. When I left his house to go my own way, his good luck token of a silver sixpence was placed tenderly in my hand. I have it to this day.

Again I was alone, with time to reflect and unravel my muddled thoughts and my tattered

Keith Low

emotions. Then I met a like mind. The next year was spent in the company of another recent escapee: Peter, a former air-traffic controller who, with too much drink and heart trouble behind him, had also chosen to stay, and paint. He took off my shoes and gave me the feel of the island beneath my feet. We spent many happy times maze-lost on the pathways, harvesting and cooking the treasures of the island and

The unforgettable view from the Seven Stones, the island pub

THE ISLAND INGREDIENT

lying side-by-side on beaches, to cloud-watch and giggle.

I still often talk of those times, the thrice-weekly strolls to the evening pub, the long-lost spectacles, and the times of wrecking on the beaches—especially the one lucky day when all of that glorious wood floated in, as if God had dropped a matchbox onto our beaches and into the hands of the gleeful islanders. The wood now adorns the houses of all, as shelf, bed, table and a gratitude for our providing sea. But we have never found the spectacles to this day: they are probably reunited to the nose of some other grateful person, hedge-found whilst cutting.

The pub the two of us frequented, the only one on the island, called 'The Seven Stones'— had been built and run by Edna and John since 1973. It was our winter meeting-place as islanders, and still is. In those days it was an austere but welcome place to meet others who came to talk of flowers, weather, and the foolishness of some poor soul who had met misfortune. Open three evenings a week in the winter, it was our oasis, although the coldness of the bar often necessitated coats, and the numbness of one's little finger was the signal for home, or yet another whisky. It was the hub of the island: in summer warm, lively and a bustle of excitement … then quiet, humorous and reflective on those winter nights when the wind blows away the stars.

*

INEVITABLY, the rolls of London money I had arrived with diminished, and the necessities of work once again became a harsh reality. The one big tourist installation, St Martin's Hotel—'St Martin's on the Isle', to give it its full name—provided me with some work for the next season, as groundsman and gardener, and my fascination with the local flowers and fauna was fed by a period of learning and a glorious summer of outside work, brushed by the elements and educated by the land.

The sea, however, would soon provide another adventure of discovery when the skipper of a local netter, Andrew, looked for a new deckhand. The many summer holidays I had previously taken here had often been punctuated by trips out to take photographs on the *Hustler*, a forty-foot fibreglass fishing boat rescued from a sinking in Newlyn harbour. The periods of photography aboard also began to diminish as the times spent kneeling on rolling washed decks, gutting and filleting fish, increased.

Skipper Andrew Goddard

These summer hobby trips had given me a fragmentary taste of the sea and I wished to know more. The offer of a full-time job was as irresistible as it was frightening, but I joined the boat, cut the sleeves off all my sweatshirts, and bought myself a reliable alarm clock. The pace of life changed instantly.

The time aboard the boat was filled with constant activity until our exhausting day was over. We steamed home the twelve miles to the island half-sleeping on scrubbed decks, to be woken only by the oncoming smell of land. To watch the curious white shapes of gill-caught fish rise up from the depths was always fascinating, and a never-ending source of mystery—the coral and stones trapped fifty fathoms deep in the net, never seen by man before, were placed on my shelves; the monkfish cheeks, a crew bonus,

Bloggs relaxing on a rough homeward journey

stored in the freezer for leaner days. We were wet, cold, and tired, and in poor weather sometimes searched each other's faces for signs of concern, but the thrill of the hunt overrode all.

*

ON GOOD days after fishing the Seven Stones reef, we steamed with fish-bursting bilges to the mainland and to Newlyn harbour, where our catch was straight onto the market and ourselves straight into a Chinese and a can or two of burning lager. Ice-loaded, chocolate-gorged and the boat fuelled, we settled down on deck until the chill of evening air shuddered us and forced us asleep upright in the cabin, until our arrival back on St Martin's at midnight.

We'd depart the moorings at six, and our hastily-prepared sandwiches would be devoured on the hour-and-a-half steam to the first net. Weather permitting, we hauled the last net in around two at night—the homeward deck now a battlefield of fish carcass, blood, and the transparent feather-bodied spider crabs that had never before seen sun. Head-down and seagull-followed, we'd beat for home—filleting, cheeking and sorting the rejects for Mark's crab-bait pot, disturbing the surface-lain Sun fish that passed like alien craft, picking the free-floating pot buoys that had broken away from their captive ropes.

With deck scrubbed, ropes coiled and boxes hosed, we pushed sometimes two lazy dolphins with our bow wave. They occasionally swivelled to study us with a skywards eye. We breathed, smelt and exuded fish. By our very pursuit we had become part sea.

Other boats we occasionally saw. Richard with his pots on the Stones, a French trawler with wrapped propeller, whose half-naked and nut-skinned inhabitants appeared at the stern like a flock of wild-haired vampires. Lastly,

the *Provider*, whom we towed out of danger, enjoying humorous banter with her boys, only to hear she soon went down off Lundy with all hands lost. Young men.

Usually, though, it was us alone, on a vast landscape, dwarfed by the sea and the sky.

The sleep on the way home was inevitable, with the sun high, the breeze cleansing and soporific engine droning. Bloggs and I lay and merged with the deck. We would wake when we could smell the land.

The chill of waking, and the approach of St Mary's, would soon shake us back into activity. Boxing the catch, icing-in, fuelling, and a chat with the crew of *Swan Dancer* to see what her trawls had reaped.

The heat of St Martin's' land oppressed and fooled me as it moved as I walked or sat or stood. The crawled-onto bed provided a sanctuary. My underwear smelt of fish as I pulled it off.

*

SUDDENLY, the boat had to be sold and Andrew and I delivered her to the new owners at Newlyn, our outriders a pair of pilot whales, saying goodbye. I flew home jobless, sea-less and without money. The Hotel again provided the security I had once relied upon, and enabled me to continue contributing financially for my children, living in my former town, Brighton.

'Maintenance Operator': my new title. The

Women's gig at rest

work was varied but the freedom of the sea was removed. I was an employee, a cog; life was a dull fragment of how I felt. Rowing kept me alive.

The infectious agony of racing pilot gigs on the islands is something I have been honoured to be part of to this day. Six crew and a fearsomely expletive coxswain train twice and race once a week from April till September. The boats, some more than a hundred and sixty years old, are jealously and protectively guarded by those who once have sat and those who continue to sit in them. They were originally built as pilot boats to guide ships safely through the greatest boat graveyard in Europe, with the unwritten rule of the first pilot aboard the ship winning the piloting fee. They were also used in times of disaster as sea rescue vessels, carrying both people and cargo to safety from those ships unlucky enough to find one of the many thousand precipitous rocks and ledges that still find boats today.

Made of Cornish elm and approximately thirty foot long, they are raced today in celebration of the piloting tradition. The most dramatic and spectacular event is the May bank holiday World Championship race from St Agnes to St Mary's, where up to ninety gigs poise wind-chilled on a start line the breadth of a mile, waiting for the hesitant flag to drop.

The ecstatic, masochistic pleasure of rowing

'through' several gigs during such a race is pure competitive exhilaration, while the sensation of being overtaken is the slow dreamlike agony of running motionlessly.

Regardless of the day's exhaustions, once you are on the sea with oar in your hands all is forgotten, exchanged for striving in harmony, majestic. The return home under a liquid sky is a time to reflect and flex the taut shoulders, the warm glow of alcohol at times quietening, or on nights of great victory enlivening.

*

THE FREEDOM of fishing made me realise that the Hotel would and could only be a temporary moment in my time here. I realised I once again needed to enjoy self-control: once again to be self-determining and self-discovering.

Many years before, my children—one bright and early morning—had returned from their errand to Alison's baking house in Middle Town to the expectant and hungry tent with empty paper bag, save some crumbs. This was the first time in my life I asked the question, *How do you make bread?*

I cracked ajar the door of a new world and looked inside, the infinite view daunting, the impatient questions rapidly overlapping in a hungry quest to understand. Once again, I began another adventure of learning, failure, success and intrigue.

Beached at Bread and Cheese Cove

CHAPTER 2: BREAD

I had not really considered bread before. Usually it came as soldiers, serried inside sweating packets of plastic, the humidity slowly trickling down the inside, each floppy slice quickly placed into the toaster to eradicate the swarming pools of azure blue mould. The taste was irrespective of colour, the wrapping wording alluring. It too was a vessel. Cheese was laid on top and bubbled under a grill, or anaemic ham was slotted inside after the cold butter had torn the slice. In my childhood, pond-greedy ducks paddled furiously toward it, and in youth Mothers Pride was remembered squashed onto a size-sixteen hook, to poach the reed-hiding chub. The French, I had seen on bicycles with long flutes semi-wrapped under arm. The Italians, spinning pizza like a fallen satellite. Arab women, welding discs of wonder inside beehive-like furnaces; weary waiters, delivering steaming parathas to soothe after the recklessly-ordered fiery curry.

Now, flooding my mind, came rapid pictures of cottage loaves, split tins, bloomers, musket loaves … the soda breads of my Irish relatives, Chelsea buns, Bath buns, scones, absolute-gravity bread pudding studded with currants. My Yugoslav schoolfriend buttering the upended loaf before he cut our slice; the lines of cat-sat-upon hessian sacks at the mill I went to for rabbit food; the huge stone wheels, centre-bored, leaning in abandoned corners long overtaken by nettles.

I remembered the grain silo in which we secretly scrambled on a Cornish farm, the seeds lodging inside my sandals. I remembered the bales of straw we made into honeycomb dens to kiss, tight-lipped, out of parents' view; the sea-like fields of corn—bordered by buttercups that were shone on the under-chin to see if one loved butter, and the white goo that was sucked from the grains as they were squashed between finger and thumb. I can remember the trepidation of touching my grandfather's hook, too sharp for children; the pictures of shires pulling man and plough along, for what I knew not; the spiky long whiskers that grew on uneaten oats under our rabbit's hutch in our wild garden, and the grasses that were darted into my jumpover, as arrows into an American soldier's breast.

It suddenly began to make sense. The clues were all around me, the evidence discarded, forgotten, outdated and superseded; the romance long replaced with fond-told story as the distantly-seen windmill sails lay stationary, the gleaming horse-brasses adorned pub bars, and the quern stones are set into concrete paths. The fragmented images began to arrange themselves. The questions were beginning to be answered, the suspect suspected. The mystery was beginning to be solved and the terrible realisation realised.

It was now evident that both *the culprit* and *the victim* was

.

THE LANGUAGE now began to arrange itself into subliminal idioms inside my mind. A tale began to emerge:

to earn a crust

the staff of life

bread of heaven

feed me till I want no more

give us this day our daily bread

a baker's dozen

which side your bread is buttered

YOU REAP WHAT YOU SOW

make some dough

be a breadwinner

take bread out of someone's mouth

BREAK BREAD TOGETHER

oh crumbs!

John Barleycorn is dead!

the grim reaper

CAST YOUR BREAD UPON THE WATER

the catcher in the rye

the bread of confession!

patti-cake patti-cake baker's man

bake me a cake as fast as you can

we plough the fields and scatter

to sow one's oats

Mother earth

CORN DOLLY

the upper crust

and

the feeding of the five thousand.

It was everywhere, the greatest story ever: it permeated our very existence and I knew nothing about it!

*

I TALKED to people. Everyone wanted to tell their story. The master-baker grandfather. The memory of seed, grain, mills, the flour on the kitchen table; of the nosebags on steaming horses, the building of the haystack at harvest time, the loading of logs into wood-fired ovens, and the baker asleep on dusty sacks. The eagerness of their memories threw up pictures of a time erased, of olfactory ecstasy, of flavour and of expertise—their fond and longing descriptions of past fare and past times, inevitably doomed to extinction by the so-called progressing world.

I needed to know how to make bread. I needed to witness, experience and harness the wonder of humankind's first alchemy—the harnessing of a wild, untamed, microscopic, living animal. Yeast.

I began to read.

The depression that first book engendered weighed heavily, pushed me asleep on sunny trains as it became a tome of loathing. The realisation of the enormity of this new world once again highlighted my insignificance, verified my ignorance.

Determined not to be daunted, I chose a recipe and chose recklessly to ignore its banality. Even then, I ran before I could walk. The loaf that emerged was just edible but failed my high expectations. I was furious: how *do* you make bread?

I would attempt sourdough, then. The oldest of breads.

The inhalation of the chemical concoction I had alchemised evacuated the air from my lungs and liquefied my eyelids. I teetered around the lounge like a sentry gassed in the trenches. The promise of huge flavour-filled loaves was there, but once again the dense, leaden brick was apprehensively pulled from the oven; it blunted the serration of the breadknife and gave the birds a hard task for a week. I would not be beaten. I read again.

Gradually, the fruits of my oven began to resemble bread, but it still was too soft to cut and too sweet to eat. I had to rationalise my method. Walk before I ran. My approach was simplified, my ineptness acknowledged, my mistakes realised. After weeks of failure, one Sunday evening I pulled four magnificent steaming loaves from a tired oven. I was a proud father. I was a Baker, or so I thought.

We began to eat bread. It began to replicate.

Alison, the campfire supplier of bread to the hungry tent-dwellers on St Martin's, had sadly left. I remembered again the soft and warm rolls my children had sometimes returned with, the heavy cakes described as light, devoured in one sitting, and the scones topped with Christine's homemade clotted cream, my heart stopping. I saw the opportunity.

With expectant jam-jar for the takings, and a cool box to contain the bread, I delivered my first loaves, placed lovingly next to Christopher's carrots, tomatoes and courgettes. My bike clanked home in speedy anticipation. The shed approached, and so did doubt.

I arrived … and they were gone. Four one-pound coins lay appreciatively inside my jar. I was ecstatic. I had made *bread*. And I had sold *bread*.

Word got around. 'Bread with flavour, albeit a little heavy', people were saying.

Within the month, people were stopping me with gaunt eyes and hollow cheeks, those who had been beaten to the shed. The home lounge—our pride—flour-strewn, the washing-brush a dough-stick. The bowls of over-proving mixture, cling-film-welded. Bread-tins filled the sink, and a fine dust filled the air. It had to stop.

*

ACROSS the narcissus-filled field behind our house lay an abandoned granite barn with very little roof left and collapsed glasshouse attached. We looked longingly and dreamt. Investigation once again brought upon us the depression of improbability.

Built in the 1920s as a place for the manufacture and store of lobsterpots, it had long fallen into disrepair and was being gradually reclaimed by nature. Three hundred wooden flower boxes, island-made, with the inscription

J.L Goddard. Deposit four shillings

crammed the roof space as a reminder of this changing landscape and giving us respect for the past toils of generations of flower-growing islanders.

An air-raid table lay bomb-impermeable and covered with boxes of saved rolls of twine. Island thrift. The euonymus grew up through the roof where missing red pantiles had until then withstood the easterlies, and the once flower-filled glasshouse was a carpet of twinkling shards of glass and broken terracotta pots.

The hugeness of the conversion to be done and the naïvety of our knowledge admonished us. We walked home silently.

Our original project of establishing vineyards on St Martin's had fallen on stony ground. Despite support from the Duchy, suitable land was scarce, and most of it would not be freely surrendered by islanders who were reluctant to relinquish the soil that had once been their breadwinner. We were now determined as to the path we would take and would not to be daunted in our quest for independence and self-sufficiency. Despite our innocence, we knew that an island bakery could fulfil that need.

*

I COULD actually hear the incredulous smile of the Duchy Land Steward during that first exploratory telephone call, as he pondered the bizarre prospect of a bakery on an island of a mere hundred inhabitants. However, our modest predictions and persuasive pleadings were noted and not forgotten. The candlelit telephone box at Higher Town now became my office, my pockets bulging with silver coins and notepad.

The next two years of costing, pricing, planning meetings, of cashflow forecasts, letters, telephone calls, profit-and-loss accounts and researching brought us no nearer, it seemed. The Land Steward's description of myself as 'that mad Irishman' was now kindly abbreviated to 'Toby', but still the building still sat untouched. We dreamt, and doubt once again visited, as I continued to bake and burn. We persevered, and slowly began to grind them down. We could not be ignored.

Finally the belligerence, the pestering, the persistence, the persuasiveness and the power of our belief brought a Duchy representative from Buckingham Gate. He shook our hands, agreed to our requests and disappeared as quickly as he had arrived. We were thrilled, speechless, numbed and terrified. What had we done?

I quickly went to the shop for some calming whisky. The following day would see the beginning of St Martin's Bakery.

*

THE REALISATION, the fears, the worries, the conviction of our argument, the faith, and the expectations that were now upon us, were immediately and constantly tangible. To sleep was to dream bakery, to wake was to build bakery. The devotion of Terry Davies, the builder, and John Poat, the architect to the project, only heightened and highlighted the absolute terror of self-belief. The humour and toil of Andy, Dave and Rob softened the anxiety as we approached obstacle after obstacle, and overcame them.

The weather was kind to us that winter. The easterly winds were few and the sun warming as we pointed and roofed, mixing unending barrows of cement, waiting for the clattering of the cement mixers' cleaning-stones as they were tipped onto solid ground at the end of each day and the motor thankfully stopped.

We saw few people in the spring either! Those we did, those who enquired, often walked with raised eyebrow. Even the Jehovah's Witnesses were inquisitive; polite and yet fully doubtful. Dave smiled and concealed his cloven hoof.

The suspecting islanders also looked with interest at the busy project. They had seen people, ideas and dreams never realised in this unforgiving landscape. I heard many phrases, listened to many opinions, and saw many

Terry Davies

shaking heads. To retain sanity, an overriding veneer of self-belief was needed; the jaw was set, the teeth were gritted as I blanked out doubt.

Inwardly, the turmoil mutated, divided and accelerated as we neared the completion date. The building work threw at us many moments of despair, most seemingly overwhelming and conquering at the time. The location of water and its drainage on this granite lump of an island, in the Atlantic, with little or no topsoil, was a major problem, its consumption and disposal as tangible as our forecasts.

Lisa painting

We encountered a concrete doorway, impervious to the mightiest of power tools; we found a crack in one gable-end large enough to split the greatest resolve, and by our freight-boat-waiting suffered delays that one by one gnawed away at the hours left. Breakdowns of equipment, quickly and skilfully repaired with what we had available: impossible problems laterally solved by Terry's improvising mind.

In fourteen weeks, we had achieved the building of a bakery on St Martin's.

As completion neared, our immediate plans were pre-empted by our friend Lisa, the former award-winning pastrychef at St Martin's Hotel. How to bake bread in a domestic oven was the limit of our knowledge. Lisa would change that comprehensively. Donning overalls, face mask and paintbrush, she painted and varnished by day, then kneaded us into shape in the evenings with choux pastry, croissants, profiteroles, millionaires' shortbreads, Jersey twirls, flapjacks, date slices, carrot cakes, and more I cannot list. We are forever indebted.

Louise and Lisa created an opening-evening buffet of style and magnificence: flower-strewn, flour-created and fully inspired. The islanders came and admired our work with reserved judgment. The jury was still out. The last guests, however, left at three.

With a held breath, we prepared to open. After the builders' dust was cleaned, we cooked, created and baked till exhaustion took us to bed for two hours. Our first customer, at six in the morning, was an expletive-laden practical-joking Scots visitor, with heavily-tattooed arms and a fearsome mongrel, who accused our cream cakes of being stale and out of date. 'It was a good joke', he later claimed. (After ejection, he was never seen on the island again!)

We had no preconceptions of a bakery. We had visited few, save the ones on the mainland that contained the replicated pastries, bad bread and a lack of fresh yeast for sale. Our naïvety was to become our weapon, our liberating factor, and our ignorance the key to our innovation. At first, thankfully, the pace was slow. The islanders were fascinated, but still apprehensive of this as yet 'half-baked' project. The visitors remained unaware of this new diversification. We knew we had to be patient.

By degrees, visitors and islanders alike began to discover us, and we began to hear compliments amid their recollections of flavours they remembered from their distant past.

BUILDING THE BAKERY

CHAPTER 3: FIRST SEASON

'Bread alone' was not to be our battle cry. The other island bounty lay largely untapped, and by many untasted. Years before the Bakery had been realised, and with advice from Keith and from J.J. Goddard, the owner of the Seven Stones pub, I began to net the beach for grey mullet—which is the most unfortunate name for such a beautiful and succulent, but much-maligned fish. Like a firm silver torpedo, it hoovers the shoreline for insects and grubs among the tide-tossed weed. Some were soon to fall into the net.

The wonderfully fleshy and firm oily fillets they provided gave me the inspiration to experiment with different methods of curing and smoking. I cured them with a mixture of salt, sugar and fresh dill which we grew in abundance. My first poor attempts emerged as very salty, and my smoking technique rendered the fillets crisp and dry. However the flavour was fantastic.

Thus the results were fine-tuned, and the percentage of salt was adjusted, as was the length of curing time. As for the smoking material, I tried apple wood, gorse wood, and elm, before discovering the gentle smouldering of oak dust and a longer cold-smoking method.

This experimentation became another joy and the thrill of expectation remains today when I have laid the net on a spring tide and can enjoy the heavenly taste of a dill-sprinkled slither of that wonderful oak-wisped fish.

Rick Stein at the Seafood Restaurant in Padstow soon came to hear about this innovative choice of smoked fish and I was proud to supply his restaurant with cold smoked mullet for two summer seasons. I began to read avidly about the succulent Parma hams of Spain and the cured meats of Italy. The invitation to the first slow food movement's convention of worldwide small food producers in Turin inspired me to begin to cure and smoke our home-reared pork. Huge back legs were cured in a brine mixture laced with herbs and treacle for approximately twenty days before being smoked for a month with gentle oak dust. The resulting Parma-type ham emerging as a beautifully-bronzed sculpture with a deliciously soft and delightfully cured flavour. A treat to be savoured.

In the Bakery, mullet soon turned into an essential ingredient. The new discovery, smoking food, became another joy with which to experiment, and the occasional unlucky salmon was instead our lucky wild Atlantic treat.

Sea lettuce, a vivid green seaweed, used to be collected on Lawrence's, where I still set the net. I washed and dried it in an ambient oven till it was barely crisp. Com-

Toby with 'Lucky', the pregnant sow

bined with our own sundried tomatoes and feta cheese, it made into a fantastic bread which tasted of the sea and the land. I christened it the Lawrence Loaf (see p. 83).

The sea spinach that we collected on beach and shore grew in great abundance. We used it in the home to wrap chicken and pork. It was robust and delicious, and indeed rarely harvested. Its inclusion in quiches and as an iron-rich complement in soups brought a flavour of the islands, too. The wild sorrel of the pathways was also collected—a piquantly sharp citrus flavour useful in our many salads for offer—as was the plethora of plump sun-warmed blackberries, plucked with scratched and purple-dyed hands and then combined with Audrey's windfall apples to make the most delicious of pies (see p. 172).

We scoured the beaches, hedgerows and fields for anything we could reap for free. Huge shaggy parasol mushrooms, along with the ink-caps from the Hotel lawn, would provide our winter soup, some of it frozen for the following season. The cockles raked on the flats and the razor shells enticed from their holes by sprinklings of salt were enjoyed straight from the beach, gently poached and flash-fried, with a knob of butter and a slice of garlic. Audrey's box of help-yourself artichokes were cubed into a sugar solution and made into huge savoury loaves of sourdough, while the rosehips from Steve's garden made jars of syrupy sunshine-golden jelly to sell, to spread on our toast, or to make into the most intoxicating, memory-wiping wine.

Sea Spinach

Steve's partner, Colin, taught me the skills of bee-keeping, and I shall never forget the sight of the tens of thousands of bees as I first lifted the lid of the hive. We spent many evenings clouded in smoke and swarmed by concerned bees as we stole their heavy frames of honey, to be spun and emptied in the Bakery. I tried adding to a mix of wholemeal dough the honeyed water residue of the cleaning process—with spectacular action, rendering a huge lump as fluffy as a down pillow. Today we add commercial honey (mine is needed to sweeten my tea!) to all of our bread—this pure form of sugar enriching and invigorating the rampant yeasts.

The small herd of pigs we maintain also provided a source of value-added food. Fed on stale croissants and Chelsea buns, they grew happily and contentedly fat. Regulations regarding home-killed animals prevented us from selling through the Bakery, but this did not stop me from producing my own chorizo, herb sausages, bacon, pancetta, brawn, and huge sides of golden-brown Parma hams, salted and smoked as described. We feasted through the winters on these and still enjoy pork produce of such free-range quality. Other scraps are also fed to the growing flock of free-range turkeys, chickens and ducks that produce for us fantastic meat and multicoloured eggs with huge yolks of saffron orange—but which, if not discovered in some secret hedgerow hideout, lead to yet more hoards of unwanted, but adorable bumble-bee chicks.

*

THAT FIRST season for us in the Bakery was soon over. We had baked and burned and learned. The August frenzy of business had been oppressive, and the end so sudden that we had no money for the long winter ahead.

The gig rowing, three times a week, was exhausting but emancipating. A whole new version of squirrelling began. In my small punt, off Round Island, I watched the huge open mouths of basking sharks and caught mackerel by the bucketload. They were smoked and stored. Bags of blackberries were frozen bullet-like for the next year; the pork was salted away, carrot cakes stashed and the net sorted out for the winter.

I had not expected the guilt, arising from suddenly redundant time, that was soon to hit.

With the Bakery cleaned—gleaming and put to bed—we took daily walks with the dogs, who were now also transformed during my dusk or dawn forays with the gun. After the freneticism of that year, I felt hopelessly adrift, lost. I could not adjust to the freedom of the time that now stretched in front of me. It was to be another learning process: to let go, to stop, to relax— once again to soak into the island landscape.

I continued to bake three nights a week for the islanders, who now had fresh bread delivered to their door, and for both Tresco and St Agnes, who had also discovered us, but still the memory of emptiness at the onset of that first winter and the meagreness of the money we had accrued is a harsh one.

Running was my time to create, plan and compose. The winding footpaths of St Martin's allowed me the purity of mind to focus on new ideas, think of new products and prepare a strategy for the future. The barely-noticed hills and footprintless beaches gave me an invigorating escape inside myself, a time to reflect, a time to catalogue and question. Each mechanical stride was the ticking away of the mind and that brief winter.

Shima, Gaby and Jazz

CHAPTER 4: HARD WORK

*O*nce *again we were open.*
'Thankfully', said the bank.

Barney would now join the team. Working for each of the past summers in the local tearoom, as chef and waiter, Barney arrived every morning to collect their bread. Like me, he had visited St Martin's many times, his family owning a large holiday cottage next to our home.

We put the prospect to him of becoming our baker—which, surprisingly, after emphasis from me on my own self-education in baking, did not shock him too much. With much training and a baptism of fire in the oncoming season he was soon to take my place at the large dough mixer we had bought and allow me the scope to concentrate on other areas. He worked steadfastly, without complaint; and with barely a murmur he took the summer madness in his stride—in spite of the pressure, which I too had, of the relentless rowing of the gig, as well as keeping wicket on Sundays for St Martin's Cricket Club.

Today he passes on the extensive knowledge of bread he has acquired over the last five years to the pupils on our Bakery Holiday Courses with confidence and panache, and has brought a solidity and reliability to the Bakery, something that has allowed it to grow in a way that would not previously have been possible.

This too is true of the many summer workers that return each year to the Bakery, and have become part of the family. Some I have known since nappies, on the campsite. They have grown with us each year and it is a joy to see their returning pale faces, their confidence and their youthfulness. They have created niches of skill and creativity from which I am still learning and are as invaluable as their names are considerable: Louise, Ryan, Tim, Pella, Will, Halcyon, Liam, Amaranthe, Morwenna, Rosie, Emma, Elleke, Kaz, Sam and Sam, Helen, Derek, Lindsay, Patrick, Natalie, Poppy, Jenny, Marta, Sprog, Abby, Megan, Thea, Nika and Bethan, and of course my now-grown children Darcy and Sean.

We were now strong. This new strength, along with a complementary and growing reputation, was beginning to attract the confidence of people around us.

*

CHURCHTOWN farm, our employers a few years back, during the times of planning and creation and the year of kindly storing our cheaply-acquired oven, asked us to provide our first outside-catering buffet. The event was a celebration of the completion of an extensive Duchy-built centre for their postal flower business, which like ours had grown rapidly out of its own meagre beginnings. The evening was a great success. Compliments from different directions entwined and we were well paid.

Another buffet swiftly followed for Princess Alexandra, who was arriving by helicopter to open the new emergency centre on St Martin's. Many hours were spent, with extra help drafted in, to produce a buffet fit for a Princess. The day went fantastically well, except for the excited chatter of the radio-bedecked detectives, who worried about our freshly-escaped pigs turning up in tuxedos for lunch. Happily the pigs never

Toby, on the opening day of the Bakery

of a successful and enjoyable gig racing season. I shall never forget the first pig roast (we have since held many). With sun beating down, I sat with glass of red wine in my hand reading my 'Moro' Moroccan cookery book, as Radio Three played its Eastern Hour music slot to accompany the sizzling of the pig. I could have been in Marrakesh.

We have seen many moments of such size and style since. The island certainly knows how to enjoy itself.

Our reputation was beginning to be enjoyed by others. Tresco Stores began to order bread, quiches and cakes in considerable number, with Kate's cheekily mis-spelt sign above our organic loaves there announcing it as 'St Martin's Orgasmic Bread'. The pub on Tresco, the New Inn, was eager to take our large pasties, made from the homegrown Tresco beef herd. St Agnes now also ordered bread, although the logistics of delivery to the most distant island sometimes created a headache of telephone calls and required the help of some kind boatman to enable it to be delivered to their quay.

As I've said, after a letter of introduction and a posted sample, Rick Stein at the Seafood Restaurant in Padstow was highly praising of my subtly-smoked mullet. Despite my entreaties about the amount of fish we could realistically catch to supply even ourselves, we relented and began to send fish to the restaurant on a two-weekly basis. The mullet, we later found out in discussion with him in Padstow, was served as a trio of fish at lunchtime, accompanied by smoked salmon and smoked trout with a horseradish vinaigrette salad. He would later kindly include the Bakery in his *Food Heroes* book that accompanied his BBC TV series, and as I've also said, he invited me and my daughter Darcy to attend the first worldwide Slow Food

materialised, preferring the fresh grass and nose-dug roots alongside their now bare and muddy field. We were back to reality with a bump, and after a day of champagne and polite conversation, changed into more suitable clothing for pig coaxing, fencing and hammering in posts, tired.

The Bakery began to be even busier, the visitors arriving in droves, recommended by their landlords and landladies on St Martin's and the other islands. The shop was constantly full, the benches outside sat on by many contented people enjoying the sunshine, along with our food and a glass of our homemade lemonade. The weight of numbers collapsed our homemade tables, on occasions. We should have made the supports out of pumpernickel!

Other celebration events now began to follow. We provided for beach wedding parties, anniversaries, retirements, birthdays, barbeques and put on whole pig roasts to celebrate the end

St Helen's and Round Island from the Pernagie coast of St Martin's

Conference in Turin in 2004. It was an inspiring, emotional and invigorating experience for the likes of us, new to the food world. We met locust farmers from Senegal, millet growers from Peru, salt producers from Japan, reindeer smokers from Lapland and salmon farmers from Scotland, among many others.

Alongside the conference ran the *Salon de Gusto*, the Italian equivalent of the Good Food Show but on a vastly greater scale. Stalls and stalls of the regional cheeses, wine, cured meats and bounty of Italy beyond belief or comprehension of variety! Where has our own regionality gone?

*

OUR EARLY terrors of simply opening and owning a bakery on St Martin's were soon supplanted by the logistics of supply and survival. The amounts we had modestly predicted we'd sell in our initial cashflow forecasts were soon outstripped by the demand we'd created. We had to re-evaluate the supply of ingredients we were consuming, reorganise the small storage areas we had originally designed, and squeeze yet more tools and equipment into our tiny kitchen. With deliveries from the mainland and other islands sometimes unpredictable, a careful eye was kept on stock and the calendar.

Forward planning, a knowledge of how the supply routes worked, and an ability to improvise have long been good attributes of islanders, ones that have allowed them to develop, diversify and grow. At bottom, this versatility is a way of existence; by the level of their understanding of it, they sink or swim. In order to survive and be successful we had to acquire and develop these skills. We found we learnt fast!

Those that provided us with services, support and ingredients allowed us to exist and enabled our expression and growth. People were constantly offering advice, suggestions and recipes they had enjoyed or created themselves. They helped with supplier referrals, recipe-book recommendations and their stories from their past.

Our flour supplies in both cases came from people willing to help us. First there was Heygates, from Northampton, who both grow and mill, and provide us with a quality organic product, which is predictable in standard and reliability and has been a tremendous asset both from the outset and during the steeper part of our learning curve. The thirty-two kilo organic sacks distributed to us by Carters of Redruth are delivered to the Isles of Scilly Steamship Company in Penzance, who then carry it virtually to our front door.

Shipton Mill, from Tetbury, Gloucestershire, is our other flour supplier. Experts in specialist flours, they deliver organic white, stoneground wholemeal, rice flour, ciabatta, soda, spelt, rye, five-seed mix and pumpernickel flours.

This relatively recent relationship with Shipton has added tremendously to the Bakery. It has given us a chance to experiment and express ourselves through some of the more demanding recipes. I was fully aware of the British preoccupation with white bread, and it has been my constant goal slowly to try and enlighten our customers with flavour. Today the soda breads, rye loaves and rosemary ciabattas are gradually growing in popularity. Indeed, some of them have even come to be expected in the Bakery, satisfying the increasingly enlightened British palate.

Shipton Mill, neighbouring Prince Charles' estates at Highgrove, buy organic wheat from his farm. Some is manufactured into the popular Duchy Originals biscuit range. The excess they sell on to bakeries such as ours. It was a significant and proud moment, then, that when asked by the Duchy in 2002 to provide a buffet for His Royal Highness, who was on St Martin's to see the transforming work that had been undertaken since his last visit, we were able to produce an inspired spread, using our landlord's own flour.

The transport infrastructure that supports the islands is a testament to human determination to survive and achieve in this detached landscape. By their very location, at the very point at which two great trade routes separate, the islands have been an important trading post since Roman times,

Toby with HRH the Prince of Wales

with easy access to the West and South coasts, to Ireland and to the continent once Scilly's rocks are past. To this day they offer a much-visited anchorage. We see many boats from England, France, Italy, Ireland, and Spain and further-flung ports—brave and enquiring sailors wishing to visit this jewel of ours and willing to navigate the treacherous routes to safe harbour.

Transport between the islands has been shaped by necessity, has become a well-practised and visible part of Scillonian life. The passenger boats, school boats, doctor's launch, cutters, cargo ships, pilot gigs, water taxis and small punts have, since the earliest of times, woven their ways between the islands, carrying people, cargo, coffins, gigs, fish, flowers, animals, mail,

vehicles, fuel and news. They are our lifeline, and the greatest respect is owed—but not always remembered—to those who brave the cruellest circumstances to maintain taken-for-granted but vital services. No household or business could hope to exist without supply and delivery.

*

THE TEMPERATE climate of Scilly, along with its rich soils, once supported a thriving flower industry which helped shape the infrastructure of freight between the islands and the mainland. The narrow high-hedged fields were cultivated to provide a warm and protective environment to grow daffodils, narcissi, gladioli, freesias and also early potatoes. It enabled Scilly to exploit

Maderium Geraniums

the advantage of an early flower season—most narcissi are now picked in November, December and January—and beat the mainland growers to market by several weeks. The many farms employed teams of workers, both men and women, busily picking, grading, tying bunches into ten stems, and then boxing them and sending them by boat to the waiting mainland agents.

Today, the flower industry is struggling to compete with modern forcing methods, imported flowers and a ridiculously low market price. In my relatively short time here, I have seen the price of a bunch of beautifully created and exquisitely scented narcissi drop from seventy-five pence a bunch to ten pence or less—the price offered by mainland agents—and some are literally thrown away while the farmers of the isles receive a note of non-sale. The sight of Henry and Derek toiling away in all extremes, chasing the wind and weather and getting scant reward for their love and dedication, is probably—in one way sadly—a thing of the past. Most fields now lie abandoned, except for those owned by exceptionally determined and creative growers such as those who have diversified into direct mail-order supply.

The 1960s saw a large fall-off in the flower industry, along with a considerable depopulation of Scilly. The Duchy, attempting to prevent a total collapse of the islands' economy, allowed and encouraged the development of redundant buildings, some of which were once flower-workers' cottages, into holiday accommodation to supplement the farmers' meagre incomes. The islands changed again; the trend was set and the visitor numbers began to increase.

Today, approximately eighty percent of the economy of Scilly is gleaned from tourism. The visitors bask in the warm climate while the old breeds of narcissus, daffodil, lily and freesia remain largely unpicked—hedgerow-struggling still, cast aside for other flowers, largely grown elsewhere, that have become the fashion.

The *Scillonian III* ferry, once brimming with boxes of flowers, now brings increased visitors and considerable freight to the islands. Sailing from Penzance for two and a half hours, she is often followed on her dipping journey by schools of dolphins and pilot whales. The excited passengers crane their necks to see the

Henry making pots

Terry Perkins, Island boatman

ports of Newlyn and Mousehole, the perilously perched Minack open-air theatre, the dozens of smugglers' caves with their many stories, and the magnificent view of the lush approaching islands. Seasickness is not uncommon, but the physical separation from mainland Britain, the passing air and the glimpses of the plying fishing boats provide a moment to appreciate one's destination, one's new scale of time.

The slow death of the flower industry brought about the end of the *Scillonian* winter sailing and a ship was purchased from Scandinavia. Thus, during the autumn, winter and spring the *Scillonian* is laid up and the *Gry Maritha* (nicknamed 'The Grim Reaper', doubtless as a reminder for those who have travelled on her of the awfully long and rolling journey she plies!).

She is a huge, pale-blue ghost-like ship, and sails from Penzance on out-of-season Mondays, Wednesdays and Fridays loaded with freight and the very few passengers who care to suffer five hours on board. Upon arrival in St Mary's, the brave passengers are disembarked and the various cargo is sorted.

Goods for the 'off-islands' such as St Martin's are loaded onto the *Lyonesse Lady*, the inter-island freight launch, which by circular route feeds the outer communities. The crew of the *Lyonesse*— skipper Peter Hicks and one deckhand—work both the crane and the seas on a daily basis, regardless of weather and with strict observance of time and tide. No-nonsense men, chastising the slowly-backed trailer, and working with speed and care, they fill the waiting arms of the hopeful and expectant people of St Martin's on Higher Town Quay.

*

WAITING for the launch, summer or winter, is an accepted part of island life: a time to stop, talk, joke, discuss and unwind from the business of the day. Without this sometimes twice-daily collection and delivery, none of our businesses could exist, or indeed our families survive. Our bread, pasties, quiches, cakes and tarts are carried by the *Lyonesse Lady* to all of the other islands every day in the summer and three times weekly in the winter (cake-induced, of course).

St Martin's would also be adrift if it were not for the island boatman Terry Perkins and his staff, Rob, Chris and son Richard. Not only carrying islanders, visitors and freight between the islands, they often kindly deliver our boxes to other islands unless tide dictates that the launch has to visit our recipients earlier in the line.

Filled with encouragingly cheering passengers, Terry's boats follow the inter-island gig races. With the race over, our breath caught and a swift refreshment enjoyed, he escorts us safely back to the gig sheds—the supporters and the rowers to meet again later and relate each stroke, each victory or defeat, in the Seven Stones, until eviction—when further merriment and heated discussion carries on without breath in some shed or chilled beach.

The helicopters and Skybus aeroplanes that reach us from Penzance, Lands End, Newquay, Exeter, Bristol, Plymouth and Southampton are another vital link in the chain. They too constantly ferry people and freight to the islands—among them our Bakery Holiday Course participants, who are flown by helicopter from Penzance to St Mary's in the shoulder season and taxi-delivered to Terry's waiting boat. They arrive, in awe of the logistics of well-practised transport

and stunning views, to set foot eagerly on our quay, in anticipation of learning the secrets of St Martin's Bakery, and enjoying the beauty of the quiet island.

The courses we have run for the past six years were born out of necessity, for with only six months of real income to the Bakery, a winter supplement was needed. The constant struggle for survival is with us all here. The summer brings frenetic activity and good income, the winter a time for repair, repainting, and a drawing-in of one's belt.

I remembered the two days I had spent in a bakery in my sister's home town of Grenoble, in France. There I enquired, witnessed and learned so much in the time I was there, that it suddenly brought home to me the joy of learning, the satisfying revelation of demonstration and the key to our spartan and frugal winters. To teach, to edify, to demonstrate are among the most rewarding and warming experiences we possess. To witness the wonder of creation on the many faces we have seen on the courses was and still is a thrill I can only compare with the sight of my own first loaves leaving the oven those many years ago.

*

SOON THE winter rushes by, and the thrushes begin to bow at each other, rear up, fight territorially and sing aloft beaten telegraph poles, proclaiming their victory and domain. The spring arrives, a time to straighten the body after the winter winds, the rain and the frugality of the off-season. The fishermen, after a winter spent mending nets, welding pots and replacing haulers, wait for the large tides and quiet weather. With tractors, mats and a helpful force of men and women, the boats are slowly backed toward the now-crystal sea.

Their moorings checked and secured by

Mark Pender hauling pots

Dave and Jolene, the vessels bob in anticipation of greater times, and of the riches of the open sea. That first taste of Mark's spring-sunshine crab is unforgettable: the first taste of the ocean, and the harbinger of summer.

Mark's family go back a long way. The family originated from Bryher, and his great-grandfather, Ellis Pender was one of the legendary and heroic men who in 1927 assisted the stricken ship *Isabo* which had foundered on Scilly Rock, rescuing the crew in the most appalling of conditions and returning time and time again to ferry the men to safety. Mark now lives on St Martin's as a fisherman, while his father Mike does the same on Bryher. The sea is in their blood.

Mark's first boat, *William and Molly*, was named after his first children. He pushes the

Bloggs looking for the Dan Flag

weather—too often, it is sometimes said—and from April until October he can be seen to the north, east and west of the island punching tide, shooting and hauling the three hundred pots with which he catches lobster, crawfish and crab. The lobsters are held in a glass tank in his shed for choosing while his wife Suzanne picks out crab in the evenings—after her day's work with the education department on St Mary's.

She commutes by boat as Mark fishes. The crab, freshly picked, half white and half brown, is supplied to us every day, early in the mornings, before Mark goes to sea.

After we resisted the temptation to fill a warm croissant from the bulging bags, the crab is now put into filled rolls, transformed into quiches, and combined with vegetables and fresh dill to make much sought-after crab pasties.

THE ISLAND INGREDIENT

Nothing is wasted. Mark also delivers the emptied shells to us. These we bake, pulverise and boil, after adding tomatoes, fresh dill, onions, wild island fennel and garlic, to make an island crab bisque. The soup (see p. 96), dark russet and intense in its concentrated flavour, begs the dipping of a soft white roll and to be emptied to the dregs. The finished shells are once again returned to the sea and scavenged by the small fry and smaller crabs as they fall towards the sandy bottom.

*

DESPITE the island being surrounded by the sea, the availability of fresh fish can be scant. The demands for wet fish by people visiting on holiday increases as fast as the seas around us are depleting. When I was fishing with Andrew, he would fondly look back at his fishing logs

Adam Morton landing fish

of past times when the cod were plentiful and the hake as long as your arm. I point no blame, but the sight of six-inch long hake in a French market underlines the unsustainability of fish if not properly researched and managed.

The wet-fish we can manage to procure, and some shellfish we use at the Bakery, are supplied to us and the other businesses on St Martin's by Ian Mitchell and Adam Morton. Ian supplies us with huge pollack for fish and chips, turbot, brill, the occasional blue shark and monkfish galore, which I still love despite the gorging of monk during my days aboard the *Hustler*.

Bloggs, too, still fishes. He has done so all of his life, and his family before him. He fishes monk nets too, as well as trawling with his home-designed gear. On good days he may return with lobster, crawfish, monk tails, turbot and brill; on bad days, a chill, a tired stomach, and the expense of diesel. When he is lucky on his trawls, his catch is a mixture of vividly-spotted plaice, sole and huge juicy scallops, begging to be flash-fried. We fished together on the *Hustler* many years ago for a season, and I can remember us pulling him over the gunnels one cold spring afternoon after he had gone under for the second time. I never realised at the time that he had never learnt to swim, just fish.

Adam Morton, more for the enjoyment of being out there than profit, occasionally rows his small punt around Lawrence's Bay, Old Quay or Par Beach to shoot and splash for the abundant but speedily elusive grey mullet, in my opinion the best fish of the islands. Adam and his wife Fiona have also diversified their two enterprises. Little Arthur, a 'green' farm, is a well-managed and bountiful haven of vegetables, fruit, flowers honey and farm animals, developed by the large Morton family from barren land, and supplies the produce used in their café and bistro. It also

Henry returns from the sea

supplies the home-grown potatoes, vegetables and fruits which later combine with Adam's handline-caught giant pollack to produce their delicious island fish and chips, and desserts of complete island goodness.

*

THE WARM dark earth of St Martin's would also bear fruit for us so long as we kept a careful eye on the prolific weeds. Asparagus beds that I planted several years before would now throw up plump spears as early as February. What strawberries the sated birds care to leave are collected in carrier bags, combined with the clotted cream supplied to us by Sue and Tim on St Agnes, and inserted into our scones or decoratively set inside a Savarin mould. Sadly, the poly-tunnel I constructed from spare water pipe, wreck wood and cover was claimed by

the wind and took to the sky like a giant bird. We had however reaped two seasons of mouth-sharp tomatoes, basil, coriander and courgettes, growing secretly huge and plentiful enough to fill a barrel. The next poly-tunnel is soon to be erected from sterner stuff.

More wind-aware growers on St Martin's and the other islands also provide their hard-worked fruit, vegetables and herbs to us for inclusion in our recipes.

St Martin's would not be the same place without the timeless Henry. Fisherman, flower farmer and grower, he is as much a part of the island as it is part of him. A slice of our homity pie (see p. 116), studded with cheese, fresh parsley, onions and garlic, would not taste the same without Henry's potatoes. Nor would the huge skin-on chips that Paulie uses with local pollack to serve fish and very local chips at the pub (see chapter 5 and p. 128). Henry's potatoes would not pass for organic, but are merely mulched with seaweed in the darkest soil. They are nurtured, weeded, hand-dug and gathered in Henry's huge hands. He works day and night, his work a reflection of the seasons. On dark and windy winter nights his glasshouse in Middle Town is illuminated with boxes and boxes of bunched golden narcissi—banded, packed and cling-wrapped to arrive at the London markets. His autumn days are spent immaculately squaring the hedges of his toiled fields. His practised eye is the best of spirit levels. The ploughed fields he has prepared are ready to accept the sacks of bulbs hauled onto the field headlands. He is nature itself, working among and side by side with the pheasant, woodcock, snipe and partridge that glean his newly-turned soil for food and the reassurance of his kind company.

As well as growing his potatoes, tomatoes, cabbage, onions, sprouts and fields full of flowers for the winter market, Henry hand-hauls strings of five lobsterpots in the summer to make ends meet. He is a gentle giant with great strength, the best evidence of that a gig paddle snapped clean in half during a race—testament also to his brute determination. He can often be seen setting trammel nets on Little Bay for bait for his pots or the occasional wrasse to eat.

Before most of us are awake, he has already walked the windward beaches, wrecking for wood or any other bounty the sea may cast up. The week that glorious influx of thousands of lengths of six-metre Douglas fir was washed up, he stepped White Island bar time and time again, bringing back hundreds of lengths of the sea-weighted wood, on his strong shoulders. Nobody would dare to argue with gentle Henry, or his potatoes.

Paul Christopher, Tresco farmer

*

STEVE HAS been the supplier of herbs to my own business and others on the island for several years now, although today she is largely retired. She arrived on St Martin's in the 1960s, a single woman in what was then a male-dominated community. She took over a rundown farm and transformed it with bare hands and unwavering hard work—which has remained her approach to this day, growing flowers when the market price was right, cooking for visitors in the evenings, and lately cultivating plants and herbs, which have been a great bonus to us. Her fragrant fresh thyme is used in our pasties, while her swathing bushes of rosemary are used to favour the rosemary ciabattas that have now become so popular in the Bakery.

Johnny Webb

THE ISLAND INGREDIENT

Our pasties, large enough to blunt the sharpest of appetites are (along with Henry's potatoes) stuffed with the fantastic steak we buy from Tresco. I have never had such good beef. The chuck tender and in bite-sized chunks, the skirt a soft slab of prime steak, with a delicate marbling of fat to add extra succulence to our pasties. The herd, managed and nurtured by Paul and Julie Christopher, happily wanders the sunny undulating hills of Tresco, propagated by their magnificent but gentle bull Trevor. I keep my distance all the same. The fantastic flavour, born out of contentedness with the lush grazing environment, and the skilful butchering of Robert Trevarthon on the mainland, has gone into making our pasties something we are very proud of to this day, and talked about by many.

The larger joints of beef we salt for approximately ten days before boiling them with a clove-studded onion. The bright red slices are then smothered with fresh horseradish and made into filled rolls, which never stay for long in our display cabinets.

*

THE SHOPS on St Martin's also cater for the demanding and essential needs of a hungry island. They are a place to buy local produce, plus the other essential daily needs, and a place to catch up on the news. The Post Office and general store, run by Julia and Steve, is a supply cornucopia. Everything from bucket and spade to smoked salmon can be found there, along with a chat or an interesting morsel of information. Starting its life as a small shed, supplied by pony and cart, and previously managed by Daph Perkins (Julia's aunt) for thirty years, it has evolved into the comprehensive emporium it is today. The posters in the windows, scanned daily, display meetings, planning applications, jobs offered, and items for sale or wanted, and also provide illuminating insight into many local stories and island gossip.

The Hotel, once my employer, is the temporary home of several thousand guests and day-visitors to the island, during spring and summer. The Sunday lunches on the beach-like garden are a tranquil delight for me after a whirlwind week of food creation. To sit and take stock in the sunshine with a bottle of wine gives a time to relax and reflect, to enjoy the landscape, to empty and replenish the mind, sharing the thrills of the children splashing on the beach, enjoying the many brightly-painted boats arriving and leaving, and watching the slowly-moving sun cast ever-deeper shadows as it makes for Round Island and the horizon.

My other destination for sustenance and serenity is opposite my front door. Polreath Tea Rooms and Guest House—Webbs, when I first arrived—has now been brought into the twenty-first century by the new owners, with delightfully-cooked local fish and homemade cakes. My first recollections those many years ago was that of a dark, cat-shooed room where one would struggle to insert a spoon into the toffee-like tea Mrs Webb would prepare. Johnny Webb, her son, would long after sit pampered in the corner—smiling behind his crumb-laden grey beard, watching the world and remembering. He would become my neighbour and friend, and despite a lifelong fondness for whisky had the acutest of memories, recalling the names of people, events and practices long gone. We spent many late Sunday afternoons fence-leaning with secret mugs of red wine, talking and talking, I wish I had written it all down. I was being educated.

Sadly, he died three years ago. The fags got

overleaf: Fred Howell

the better of him, his beloved whisky at the end denied him. I still miss him waiting in anticipation, clockwork-like, in his garden every day for the *Scillonian* to clear the back of the Eastern Isles—with the repeated checking of his watch to see if she was late or early. 'There she is, on time today', he would say, with expectant relief, and return to feed Merlin. His jet-black, one-eyed, one-eared cat of this name, who would lap-sit and fix you with his friendly terror and undulating purred stroke is sadly no more either, but I'm sure his children live on, somewhere.

The art galleries of the island, diverse in their approach and interpretation, provide for us all great insight, reflection and celebration of our rich environment. North Farm Gallery was established by Sue Lewington. Self-taught, she has become a collected artist, chronologically and chromatically capturing the many moods and many changes she has seen since they took on North Farm and established a much-pilgrimaged gallery. Her books beautifully represent the prosaic, frozen moments, the daily happenings and the fleeting atmospheric splendour of this bewitching landscape.

At Ashvale Farm, Lower Town, the former house of Fred and Polly Howell, which I knew from my first holidays on St Martin's, Patrick also paints. His depictions of the untameable land and wild sea constantly emphasise the space of our environment, and the scale of our own humanity beneath our sky and the influence of the surrounding sea. His infinite stretches of tide-revealed sand containing long-abandoned boats are a reminder and testament to our fleeting influence on this land- and seascape.

Fred Howell has left his mark at Old Quay

CHAPTER 5: A NEW CHALLENGE

It was now eight years after the surreal encounter with our belligerent first customer, the fears of failure and the bread-burning a long-distant memory. (Bake and burn was our education.) We had survived, replicated, enquired and grown. Food was in our veins. We had taken on many challenges, some small, some daunting in their magnitude. The Bakery had grown in stature and reputation. The islanders and returning visitors had come to expect the same exacting standards of quality and variety we had set ourselves.

Chelsea buns

under new management. The food was prosaic and bore no reflection of local specialities, and the décor was depressingly drab. The austere atmosphere had returned and we began to think. After an ideas-crunching holiday in Tuscany, we decided to make

A new challenge was placed in front of us. The Seven Stones pub had been for many years and will long remain the hub of the St Martin's community, in ways I have described already: a place of local discussion on quiet winter evenings, a meeting place for the variety of clubs and associations we have on this tiny but organised island, and during the summer a buzz of visitor bustle. A chance for all to re-meet, to talk of children's fortunes, to share some sadnesses about those that have not returned, and a place of heartfelt embrace in genuine friendship.

Darcy had worked for the new owner in the summer season as the pub began to struggle

an approach. The new owner, without the support of his mainland-bound wife and family, agreed to meet and expressed a desire to drop the reins. Six months of secret negotiation followed, in a locality where to conceal one's toothpaste is an achievement.

Liz, my former wife and the mother of my two children, would provide some capital by selling her house in Brighton. As a social worker in Brighton, she had seen enough of desperate and tortuous court cases involving defenceless children to wrack any heart. I would try the heart of the bank for the rest.

With a strong local reputation established by

the Bakery and a sound but creative business plan to present, we were accommodated. The new terror began.

The repayments were to be exacting, the catalogue of repair, refurbishment and remodelling once again daunting. Nonetheless we accepted the challenge with enthusiasm and realised that success would only be achieved from a strong footing. Darcy, with her experience of bar work, would manage the alcohol side of the business. Liz, with past bookkeeping experience, would organise the accounts, wages and banking. I would apply myself to the marketing side of the business, and the bakery would supply breads, biscuits, desserts, pasties and food for buffet and celebration occasions.

We realised that the only approach to food that showed integrity was local sourcing. We had to find a like mind to run the kitchen.

Paulie (Paul Websdale) was a friend from earlier who had risen through the kitchens at St Martin's Hotel. From there, he had gone on to work for Michael Caines and Martin Burge at Whatley Manor. A young man, passionate about food, and with an unquestionable loyalty. I located him in Poland and made him the offer.

He hesitated for a full five seconds before firing off a clip of questions about the job. We both knew he would accept, and in later discussions he has referred to his return to the islands as 'coming home'.

Little did he know what awaited him, but true to form he arrived at four on a Saturday afternoon and was by five in his kitchen and restaurant—paintbrush, pot and pint in hand, transforming the Seven Stones into his domain. I myself reluctantly painted, scared to claim. We opened at eleven the following morning with wet walls, every table reserved (some to prevent paint getting on clothes) and to a Sunday lunch

Paulie

of unexpected busyness—the patio and decking full, every inside table taken, a visitor's friend playing jazz piano for food and beverage and a brief spying mission from the Hotel manager. He left his drink half-finished.

The realisation and shock that greeted me on our first service the following day was like living inside a dream. So overwhelmed was I by the vastness of what we had done that the morsel of food probed into my mouth by Paulie upon my arrival was neither recognised nor tasted. Sweet or sour could not be derived from it, so preoccupied was I.

Was this a foolish dream? It was only the boundless enthusiasm, energy and humour of Darcy, Paulie and Liz that gave me grounded sanity. Local food was going to be the key to success in the dining department. Paulie's love of cooking fish was to be rewarded by island fishermen willing to help our business unleash the awaiting, largely untapped flavours.

*

EASTER arrived, with a frenetic production of hot-cross buns at the bakery and armies of

"**M**y love for the islands started years ago, when I first travelled over here on a day trip with my parents while we were on holiday in Cornwall.

"St Martin's Hotel, which I came to first in 2002, was my first proper kitchen. Head chef Stewart Eddy taught me a lot, and it was here that my love of food and local produce started. After never really having worked with fresh fish, I was suddenly in a kitchen where islander Mark Pender would bring fresh lobsters and crabs into the kitchen—and the same evening they would be on the plate.

"This blew me away! Coming from pubs where I just reheated everything, it was all new to me, cooking everything to order—lobsters, fish, quail, pigeons ... the list goes on—but it was exciting and different. Over the next eight months, I realised that my life and career had taken an exciting and positive turn. By the end of the season I had worked in, and taken control of, the hot and cold larder section and the vegetable garnish section, and had done 'fish prep' on the freshest fish.

"I knew that after this kitchen I would be ready to move on into bigger kitchens, and that took me away from St Martin's.

"It came right out of the blue, therefore, when I received a phone call in a sports bar in Poland Christmas 2006. Somehow you don't expect these calls when you are in a remote location! Coincidentally, though, I was out with Marta, an old friend from when I worked on the island in 2004. Toby called me and said he had a proposition for me, and that I should give him a call when I got home.

"A whole month later, as I sat watching the programme 'Island Parish' on the TV—which featured St Martin's—I remembered that I owed Toby a phone call. He spoke of the pub deal and asked if I was interested in the job of chef.

"I was excited at the chance of going back to Scilly. It would be good to see familiar faces again and meet the new ones. To take control of my first kitchen was exciting, and I began at once to think of who or what I would need to help me through the season. I asked Kris and Lydia, a Polish couple who had worked with me up in Scotland, if they'd like to come and work with me again. Meanwhile, I'd talk with past and present chefs for their ideas and help. All this gave me a week before I was to go to Toby and explain my ideas and menus."

PAULIE WEBSDALE

visitors and islanders curious at the offerings provided by the new owners of the pub. The bar and the kitchen at the pub looked like the bastions of soldiers at Rourkes Drift, amazed at the Zulu-proportion attack.

Plates and glasses were charged, cleaned and then recharged, orders for regrouping adhered to, barrels and pumps primed, and then uniforms dusted down as the preparation began for the next attack. They stood firm and strong, as it was to be for the next conceivable time. A relentless onslaught, a weary time of hard work and humour. At the end of each day the fires were quelled, the flag lowered and the plans for the next strategy discussed.

*

THE SUMMER, albeit a poor one, brought the regular returning visitors, those with whom I had shared the beaches of St Martin's and suppers on the campsite, along with my children, many years ago. Like all returning visitors, they were aware and protective of their dear island. In the Seven Stones, to improve on the previous year was not difficult, but to compete with the other business on the island a folly. We had set our vision, and the only competition was to be self-competition: our own concept of integral living.

The décor was substantially improved and the atmosphere given our identity. The food also had to reflect our new approach. Locally-sourced food was indeed the only way, but the price of drink and food a great leveller with people who had made substantial expenditure to arrive here, or who had chosen to live in this riches-to-poverty landscape.

Paulie and his dedicated brigade of Kris and Lydia in the kitchen created exquisite dishes which brought people back time and time again. Quite often, the menu board names did little justice to the creativity, ingenuity and skill or the

Toby with salmon

years of learning invested in their concept. Darcy's boundless warmth, hospitality and inimitable homemade raspberry liquor, a Tuscan recipe she discovered some years ago, proved a perfect complement to food and a convivial evening.

Liz held the whole ship together, a visitor to this island since her conception; knowing, resolute and determined. The administration of this whole business was unlimited: the accounts a tangled warp and weft of many departments, many suppliers and also many cheques, the accelerating process of this business something to try to grasp with present and future hands; the whole enterprise a huge responsibility and task.

The feverish activity of July and August stretched us to breaking point. Glasses, plates,

Stormy December day

knives, employees, ingredients, gathered and gleaned … cleaned and prepared as quickly as we could. Days became mere breakdowns of hours, social engagements a tough battle between work and rest. A tired sofa dropped onto and a bottle of wine opened. Sleeping became a motionless activity with no dreams, only broken by the alarm to signal another shift, another motion of production.

And as swiftly as it had begun, it was over.

The increasing yellow patches on the campsite began to reflect past inhabitancy, the tripper boats began to ferry only birdwatchers eager to spot the rarest of migrating birds, and the fields of salad and vegetables were at last cleared, groomed and prepared to accept the crops for the next growing cycle.

*

As the passage of time is inevitable, the friends and colleagues of years depart. The sun lowers and the season begins to come to an end. A plethora of destructively late and humorous farewell parties begins, early quay goodbyes end and telephone numbers are fondly exchanged.

The autumn leaves pave the road for those that have worked with us, heading for their fantastic adventures bountifully saved for. Only their echoing footsteps remain.

It's now time for the winter pulling-in of belts, the taking of stock and the hatching of the new plans for whatever will be the next exciting chapter.

*M*artin ('The Reverend') Bond, a friend of fifteen years, and his son Joel fish from the *Marauder*, a thirty-nine foot trawler berthed in St Mary's. They skirt the islands and supply us with monk, John Dory, dovers, lemons, meigrim, plaice and squid for mouth-watering calamari dishes. Joel and crew fish while Martin and his wife Skinny sell throughout the islands. Born on St Martin's, from a long line of islanders, Martin has always been on the sea in one vessel or another. He once described fishing as 'not really work, is it?'.

The thrill of discovery stays with him, as it has with generations of his family.

I found him recently against St Mary's harbour wall with a handful of exploded fanbelts; he had limped back to St Mary's harbour with no hydraulics to steer by, but still with a smile to tell the story.

Ian Mitchell of St Martin's and Newlyn also supplies us with quality local fish. The skipper of a sixty-foot netter birthed in Newlyn and the owner of a thirty-foot boat out of St Martin's, he fishes monk nets to provide us with thousands of pounds of crab meat that he and his island-born partner Mandy pick out in the evenings. He is

Martin Bond with trawl

Martin and Joel Bond's boat Marauder

prolific, and like all of our suppliers provides us with his catch, whatever it may be. You cannot catch fish to order and this guarantees a varied and daily changing menu. It also gives Paulie the opportunity for creative experiment. New dishes, new ingredients, new challenges. Ian often lands us brill the size of dustbin-lids, huge turbot and monkfish. Setting gill nets on the Seven Stones reef, he brings home boxes of pollack and cod for our fish and chips. The occasional blue shark is also one of the fish he has landed—at Paulie's direct behest, for a shark dish he has learned in Australia.

Paulie and Kris in the kitchen relish the opportunity to prepare the freshest of catches, and the varieties they have never had the opportunity to deal with, some still flapping in the fish boxes heaved onto the kitchen floor. The delight with which they show me the prime fish which has been delivered is a testament to their dedication and enjoyment of food. Ian and Mandy are regular diners at the Seven Stones, savouring their hard work and the kitchens' ingenuity.

*

PASSION in one's art is a necessity for success. Our passions have helped attract many people with a dedication and drive for their work to join us in our achievement and success. To complement the cornucopia of the seas, we have the skills and obsessions of Ian Metcalf, the most prolific of growers on the island and son of a former Seven Stones landlord. He was given his first plant at three years of age and spent his schooldays growing and selling to schoolfriends and their families to supplement his pocket money. He was later educated at horticultural college in New Zealand, and after returning to work with his father in the pub has established a thriving and expanding growing business on this island.

He skilfully and steadfastly plans the successional seeding of the many variety of salads, vegetables and herbs to supply us and many other

above: Ian Mitchell
opposite: turbot supplied by Ian Mitchell

ISLAND GARDEN: *Clockwise spiral from bottom left: globe artichoke, raspberry, dill, sage, chives, flower of courgette, basil, mizuna, okahijiki, rosemary, flowerpots, coriander, Jerusalem artichoke.*

businesses on St Martin's throughout the entire season. He has tirelessly worked to turn four fields abandoned to time and irrepressible nature into neatly-groomed and bountiful pieces of rich dark soil. The chicken, horse and cow manure he collects to feed the land are added to chipped hedge cuttings and cook slowly under reclaimed carpets, releasing a slow volcanic steam.

The variety he grows gives the kitchen a vast range of island fresh-tasting produce literally grown at our door. Much produce started by hydroponic germination is then tenderly out-planted directly into the tilled earth or into cloches to protect them from wind, bird, or sun. Some plants remain in their cloches for most of the summer. Forests of sweet-smelling basil bulge under the polythene, dripping with condensation, as does the very different Thai basil, planted at Paulie's request following his culinary cookery holidays in Thailand, Australia and New Zealand (see pp. 123–4).

The exceptionally early spears of asparagus break through the ground as if by magic on February mornings, later followed by his mangetouts, fine beans and prolific courgettes, hiding and desperate to grow to marrow stage.

Successional salads cover one entire field. Lollo Rosso, Little Gem and Kos lettuces plus mizuna, next to row upon row of coriander, chives, sage, parsley, feathers of dill, rosemary to accompany our lamb dishes and okahijiki, a Japanese succulent and type of samphire used by Paulie to garnish his chicken.

Windbreaks are created everywhere by careful hedge maintenance, and permit the planting of Jerusalem artichokes, used for soups at the pub, and for the asparagus and artichoke quiches in the Bakery. Baby carrots line another field

Ian Metcalf, with asparagus

Ice cream production by the Hicks family, St Agnes

boundary; those not to standard are enjoyed by the pigs. Ian's plans are naturally for expansion and experimentation. He is constantly looking at new methods of production, looking for new varieties and digging into the past for specimens that have long been abandoned and gone out of fashion. His grubby hands are always busy.

For years now, Tim and Sue Hicks of St Agnes have milked their herd of eleven Jersey and Ayrshire cows to produce island yoghurt, butter, and the best of clotted creams. Two years ago they diversified their business with the help of returning son Sam and his wife Laura to produce St Agnes ice cream at Troytown Farm. Many years ago, I had bought their surplus milk during the winter to experiment in cheesemaking. After an initial scare, with my old friend Peter Bray, of nearly burning the Bakery down, I had stabilised the process and begun to produce cheddar and blue-veined cheese of reasonable but varying quality. Now with every drop of milk needed for ice cream, my rennet days are over.

The flavours of the ice cream they provide for us at the pub are both varied in creative flavour and exceptional in standard. The cows happily wander the fields (and sometimes the downs of St Agnes, if a hole is found in the wall!), in fresh Atlantic breezes, grazing on the lush green grass enabled by the prolific sun. After the cows are milked at dawn and dusk, the milk is set aside for butter-making, yoghurt, clotted cream or the inimitable ice cream.

With a summer staff of eleven to keep up with demand, the ice-cream plant continuously churns out an irresistible frenzy of flavours: Madagascar Vanilla, Baileys, Banana and Cinnamon, Strawberry and Papaya, Pistachio, Strawberries and Cream, Ginger, Coffee, Coconut and Chocolate and Hazelnut, Forest Fruit Sorbet and Lemon Sorbet, just to mention a few. With almost five hundred litres consumed by our happy visitors, they are a delicious treat on their own or enjoyed as a complement to the desserts created by Paulie, and the lemon tarts, treacle tarts or apple-and-island-blackberry pies that the Bakery supplies to the pub.

"After the 2002 season at the St Martin's Hotel, I went to work for Michael Caines, and then to Martin Burge's kitchen at Whatley Manor. For three months I worked in the cold larder section, but then I had a near-fatal car crash, with swelling to the brain, collapsed lungs, and glass in my hands and right eye. I was given a thirty per cent chance of recovery. With the support of my family and all the staff at the hotel, I was out of hospital ten days later, and off work for just seven more weeks.

"A month or so passed after my return from the car crash. I knew there was something wrong. I'd lost the love I'd had for my job. I didn't enjoy the hours which come with working in a top hotel. It was a new feeling for me. I'd always loved my job, regardless of the hours, but this was bugging me. I decided to hand in my notice, but not until after Christmas. I owed it to everyone for being so supportive of me.

"I would go home every night not sure what I wanted any more. I would talk with another chef who I lived and worked with at Whatley. The guy was called Ben Jenkins. I owe a lot to Ben, as he was the first at the scene of my accident, and still has a look of disbelief to this day that I'm OK and have no long-term injuries. We would talk about everything: work, life, and what I really wanted out of them.

"I wasn't even sure if I still wanted to be a chef. I had a lot of soul-searching to do. I would drive back up to Hull and talk with my parents and friends. I had to admit that I was feeling really lost.

"In my local pub, the Rattlebone Inn in Sherston, I used to talk over a pint or two to a guy who was a shrink. As we spoke, I realised that over the last year and a half of my life, I had lived at six different addresses. Yet I would always talk with special feeling about my times on St Martin's. It was he who suggested I go 'back to my home'. The phrase was powerful.

"Stewart Eddy, head chef at the St Martin's, had always helped me in finding jobs and is a great influence on my career. After taking a couple of months off, travelling around the country catching up with friends and eating in some of the top restaurants, I found myself coming back to the Scillies for a second season."

PAULIE WEBSDALE

*T*hose of us that reside here are proud and honoured to be part of the vast and varied history of these islands. The immensity of the past and the stories of early generations struggling to survive on this remote archipelago places one's own fleeting existence in a stark and fragmentary context. The evidence of settlement since the bronze ages can be seen all around us today. The standing stones and burial cairns composed of huge slabs of granite remain across Scilly and Penwith, largely intact and resolute, monuments to the past, to humanity's struggle with nature, and to the endless quest to understand this impressive landscape and its destiny. Among them, the three stones mentioned in the prologue to this book emerged from the sand a few years back. Now they have gone again, symbols both of permanence and of impermanence.

Scilly has only split into the islands of today within the last two thousand years. Once it was a land mass covered with oak and elm. It has seen the rising and relentless sea erode and encroach to create a patchwork of some two hundred islands and rocks. Just five remain inhabited today.

THE ISLAND INGREDIENT

The field-boundary walls of past generations now lie submerged beneath the turquoise seas and are a testament to the constant battle with nature and the elements. It is this story of a struggle for survival which has shaped Scilly and moulded its inhabitants into resilient and enterprising players in a picture board of visible history.

My own insignificance in the story was clearly defined for me in my first week, when I was asked to make documentary photographs of tar deposits revealed on Par Beach on an extreme spring tide. The shards of wood and deer-tooth prised from the vast and solid tar bed, a deposit and remnant of a once-verdant woodland, were carbon-dated to 2000 years BC. To hold in one's hand a piece of history four thousand years old was a quietly humbling experience, and it firmly reminded me of my fragile place on this granite outcrop.

The Romans came here quite late; the earliest coin discovered is dated 69 AD. Their diet consisted of oxen, horse, sheep, goat, fish, the common frog, rabbits, and limpets gathered from the rocks. Evidence of limpet middens is uncovered by many building projects and can

Stone Fence

Hustler. *Sunset, Old Quay*

The impressive castles on Tresco (King Charles's being sacked and then dismantled to build Cromwell's) are testimony to the historically strategic importance of the Isles of Scilly. Their siting indicates another of the deep harbours in the islands besides Hugh Town, which is the principle anchorage today. At the gateway of the English Channel and the route towards Bristol and the Irish Sea, the situation of the islands guaranteed a constantly-changing populus, and the family names suggest influx from many areas of England, Wales, Ireland and Scotland. The temperately-warmed land, foreshore and sea would feed the inhabitants during the principle periods of occupation, although starvation and famine were always on the horizon.

also be discovered along eroded cliffs on all of the islands. Limpets, an easily-gathered form of food, have been the diet of countless generations of settlers, along with further fish and shellfish from the surrounding shores.

As a twentieth-century refugee from the mainland, I am not by any means unique on

St Martin's. Each one has found his or her own means of survival, and other tales of breaking away to Scilly throw my own into interesting perspective. Recently this was demonstrated to me by a radio interview I conducted with one such refugee, who brought his own unusual expertise to the islands. Thus it was the importance of Scilly's industrial heritage that was highlighted to me in discussions with Colin Daly.

Arriving on St Martin's from London in 1971, Colin found employment on a flower farm with a resilent and hardworking lady, also from the London area, called Steve, the person that he would later marry, and my herb grower today. She had arrived some years before and begun the conversion of a broken-down flower farm and homestead that she would eventually name 'Breakaway'. Colin, with his past employment

as an industrial chemist, explained to me the importance of Scilly for the glassmaking industry in this country.

It was in 1685 that the discovery of soda ash, a vital component in glassmaking, could be extracted from seaweed, especially kelp. The Scillonians were the first people in the country to perfect the art of collecting kelp with horses and donkeys at low tide—drying, burning and extracting the vital soda ash. This industry began on the westerly end of St Martin's and next-door Tean, the seaweed being dried on the clifftops and the weed incinerated in round granite kelp pits, which can still be seen in many locations, with the blackened sand surrounding them a layer of industrial history and an indication of a hard, noxious and difficult employment and livelihood.

The resulting soda ash was sent away for use

Eastern Isles across the cricket pitch and Par Beach

in the glass-manufacturing industry. For a family to survive, they neeeded to collect some 264 tons of seaweed; for this much would provide them with an annual income of ten pounds. This method of soda-ash extraction migrated northwards to the higher reaches of the west coast of Scotland and became of vital economic benefit to small, often-impoverished communities.

Towards the end of the eighteenth century, it was discovered that soda ash could be extracted directly from seawater. Thediscovery devastated the islands and a great period of destitution, poverty and hardship followed. Begging demands for bread to feed the islanders were made to Parliament. The deprivation was the greater because increasing restrictions on the slave trade were also damaging income that islanders achieved through smuggling of different kinds. It was for this reason that the person who in 1818 persuaded Parliament to forward £500 and a supply of salt (for preserving) to keep the islanders from starvation was actually William Wilberforce, the anti-slavery campaigner—although there was general public subscription too. That year, London raised £4600 and Cornwall £2000.

Today, with my curing activities, salt is still part of island life! The Bakery is also unusual in returning to seaweed for a new reason, that of culinary ingredient.

Two hundred years ago, far-sighted men such as Augustus Smith on Tresco noted that the warm winters of Scilly would allow the production of vegetables, fruits and flowers far earlier than many mainland environments. With improvements in sea transport, the new industry of Scilly would be the exportation of early pota-

toes and, especially, flowers for the London markets. The *Scillonian* and its predecessors carried flowers every day in the flower season, which was from October or November to February or March, including flowers held back for Mothering Sunday and others (especially white flowers, held back for St David's Day and Easter). The flowers went on by train not only to London, but to Bristol, Cardiff, Sheffield and Glasgow.

Once again, Scilly saw a revival. Yet the fragility of the islands' economy is demonstrable even in recent times. Over the past twenty-five years, the diminishing returns from the flower harvests have had a significant effect on the shape of economics within the islands. The vast improvements in global transport and modern farming methods have largely erased Scilly's early season market advantage and excluded all

but the most competitive growers, such as those who have expanded into the mail-order business. Many farmers now struggle with increasing overheads and decreasing returns to send their hard-picked crops of flowers away. The majority of the narrow high-hedged fields lie abandoned, while dwindling numbers of ancient varieties of beautifully-scented narcissi and daffodils are a reminder now of how quickly fashion and the world changes.

Many farmers like Colin and Steve began to convert buildings once used for agricultural purposes into small accommodation units to supplement their meagre incomes. Tourism began to be the main source for many families who had struggled for a regular income for many years.

Adaptability is vital, and my own versatility

Looking towards Chapel Down and the Daymark

is just one example of the ingenuity required to survive. Colin, however, has showed his value to the island in an unusual and lasting way.

Throughout most of the twentieth century the electrical power on the off-islands had been provided by generators. They were noisy, difficult to maintain, and could only provide 2–3 kw of power—generally during the daytime and early evening. As the price of oil soared, they quickly became an anything-but-economic means of power production. If the islands were to sustain a modern community, mains electricity had to be introduced.

It was Colin who saw the possibility of convincing the powers-that-be to provide the power supply the off-islands needed. Since his arrival on St Martin's, his approaches to the electricity board to provide mains electricity had

been falling on deaf ears. However, his research among the archives of Parliament revealed an Act of 1899 which outlined the right of six or more people to demand the provision of mains electricity in isolated communities. A protracted campaign began in 1981.

After lengthy negotiation, the Board recognised its responsibility to lay underwater electricity cables and comply with the provisions of the Act. The Duchy was also persuaded to provide the funds to lay the cables underground on the islands so as not to ruin the unique landscape. Thus in 1986 Prince Charles, as Duke of Cornwall, officially switched on the power on St Martin's and the generators fell silent for the last time. Now, it is only when a local power failure is experienced that the realisation of the importance of electrical power to enable this commu-

nity to survive is brought home to us all.

The provision of mains electricity was also to have a large effect on the economic and social development of St Martin's. Businesses were attracted and began to establish themselves on the island—neither Bakery nor Pub could have flourished in the generator age! The influx of many new people attracted to establish these businesses, or work in them, brought young people to St Martin's, people who would play a vital role by settling and having families of their own.

This generation of a new community on the island has had both economic and social benefits, and has allowed a balanced and growing population to accumulate. The next step in this continuing story of how to develop a vibrant community has been the provision of low cost sustainable and affordable housing, a

matter for which the Council and Duchy are still today striving.

*

IN THE story of Scilly, always the sea provided and the sea took away. The multitude of rocks, reefs and treacherous tides around the islands has counted for hundreds of boats and thousands of people lost at sea. Piloting

Turfy Hill

boats into island safety or rescuing stricken ships, men and booty were part of Scillonian history. Pilot gigs were launched whenever an incoming ship was sighted, and the first gig to reach the nervous ship would board their pilot to navigate the ship to safety, or would be used to help stricken ships' crews to safety (while of course making advantage of any carried cargo). The gig tradition still goes on today in the form of interisland gig racing, on Wednesday and Friday evenings, in honour of these brave and fearless men who would forsake any element for enterprise, or assistance.

The story of the wrecks and disasters on Scilly's coast is a romantic one and has spawned modern commercial and tourist diving industries. Yet the story of Scilly's and England's attempts to lessen the dangers of its shores is, like its on-land industries, one of ingenuity and hard work, from the building of Daymark on St Martin's in the seventeenth century to the automatic lighthouses of today (see p. 2).

The destruction of the flagship *Association* and three other navy ships on the western rocks off Scilly in 1707, with the loss of one thousand

four hundred men, was to have importance on a national, global and historical scale. Many maritime disasters were based on navigational errors, and Parliament offered the huge sum of £20,000 to any person who could accurately fix longitude and so help prevent disasters of such magnitude.

John Harrison, who had trained as a clockmaker, was the man to change the face of navigational history. He produced seaworthy clocks and eventually, with improved methods of tempering steel for the mechanism's spring, manufactured a hand-held timepiece which could accurately keep time to one third of a second per day. Indirectly, he had produced a method to fix longitude, the discovery that had eluded so many, and one that revolutionised sea and also eventually air travel.

Disasters still happen, and a relatively recent one both brought the Scillies into much greater profile within Britian, but also effectively gave the island pub its name.

The Seven Stones rocks are one of the many treacherous reefs, lying just under water approximately seven miles north-east of St Martin's, and marked by the Seven Stones lightship, a red unmanned and anchored boat which can be seen during the journey to the isles. Its white light is seen emitting three times in each minute. Despite the lightship, the Stones have claimed over fifty ships to date, but the most recent and the most famous loss was that of the biggest crude oil tanker of its time, the *Torrey Canyon*. At 120,000 tons capacity, 300m long and with a draught of 21m, she was a state-of-the-art tanker, capable of cruising the world to take on and deliver her cargo of crude oil.

Pernagie Bar

hearsed attempts to bomb her from the air with incendiary devices, plus hastily-erected booms in the turbulent water, couldn't prevent her from spilling her cargo—to be later, most sadly, washed up on the coasts of Cornwall and France.

The islanders of Scilly watched with worry and horror from the clifftops, St Martin's being the nearest habitation to the Stones; crude oil was one piece of sea booty they most surely didn't desire. But luckily, due to wind and tide, Scilly remained untouched. The *Torrey Canyon* story over, Scilly dropped again out of the headlines.

On 18th March 1967, owing to a navigational error, she struck Pollard Rock on the Stones, and after spending several days breeched, and despite attempts to tow her off, she split into two. Unre-

The St Martin's of generators, greenhouses, flower distribution by boat and unmade roads was a quiet place except for its generators and had few social spaces in which the community might congregate: church, chapel and reading room was its limit, apart from the post office. It was in

THE ISLAND INGREDIENT

1973 that John Goddard, and his family, started the building of the Seven Stones pub. Using an old barn as a basis, the island pub was created and named after the infamous rocks that had claimed so many lives.

The wheel comes round. A decade later I would be fishing as crew for his son on the Stones in the *Hustler*. With the hold awash with fish we would beat on, to land her catch in Cornwall, dodging the huge tankers like the *Torrey Canyon*, and cargo ships ploughing their way along the separation zone that now runs between Scilly and the mainland. We prayed for good catches and the price advantage of landing directly at Newlyn market

and loading with fuel which we did not have to pay freight on, but inwardly secretly dreaded that extended leg to the mainland.

Later, but before I bought it, I was again to try to earn a crust courtesy of the Seven Stones. This time it was helping to cook and wash many, many pots and dishes in the pub kitchen. There was a different dread too, with the picture of the red lightship, named after the Stones, warning sailors of their concealed position. It still adorns the pub wall as a stark reminder of the perils of both employment and self-employment: of the challenge of survival in this bewildering environment.

Great Bay and White Island with Frenchman's Graves, a name from sadder days

THE ISLAND INGREDIENT

S apphire, *the last tripper boat, heads from St Mary's* through seasons of mists and carefully picked-out ledges to collect the last visitors of the season from the Island. This final departure becomes a poignant time, one for us to draw breath, relax and reflect on the first season of this new joint venture.

The final passengers embarked, *Sapphire* heads back to St Mary's and carries away the honoured people that have discovered the beauty of St Martin's: the unspoilt beaches, the endless breathtaking pathways and the timeless landscape of this jewel in the ocean.

Lower Town Quay invites the autumn sunset and the incoming of quiet water, soon to be battered by the rages of winter seas.

This is *our* time now, a time and a moment to relax and investigate; to discover and experience once again our island, to make some sense of reality of this venture we had begun. It had become our time to arrange and place some context on the frenetic activity of the season's height, to plan for the long delightfully gentle winter and assemble some strategy for the following season, which we realise will inevitably be upon us before we have time to think.

But now for our own sanity we arrange our reward and respite. Barney—the resilient, reliable and tireless night baker at St Martin's Bakery—heads off to enjoy normal periods of sleep and habitation, and to see long-lost friends and family in the Midlands, where his family have farmed for generations.

Paulie heads east to the Czech Republic, India, Thailand and China, to enjoy food and to cook in distant restaurants, which will enable him to learn new skills and sharpen his edge; to bring a

different twist to the recipes he has added to his vast repertoire here at the Seven Stones.

Darcy and partner Steve head west, to relax and discover the foods and culture of the Caribbean. Liz takes a well-deserved break from endless, depressing and mountainous bookkeeping and financial worries. Sean and I undergo essential repairs and then I head once again for Tuscany, which I had discovered with Darcy many years ago … to run the pathways dotted with fresh wild boar and deer prints, discover the natural simplicity of regional Italian food, drink deep red viscous wine and begin to make some written sense of our experiences. Later I return home, recharged, to walk the now footprint-less beaches of Lawrence's Bay and Par Beach with the dogs again, the cowries collected in my pocket.

We have made our mark at the Seven Stones: improving, embellishing and improvising as the daily events have confronted us with new challenges, discovered shortcomings and the need to think and be creative quickly. The battle for survival has come to the end of the first round, and we have been advised by our seconds and prompted by our small experience to recognise that the frenetic summer and early autumn will soon be replaced by the void of quiet evenings, few customers and a very long winter. Once again, we shall draw in the belts and immediately plan for the onslaught of a new, soon-gaining season.

People often ask, 'What on earth do you do in the winter there?' The answer is, very little: we are all too busy doing things long postponed. Unbelievably, there just isn't the time or the situation in which to do much. We are all just too involved investing in quiet moments; busy catching up with our own lives, our own battered existence, our long-overdue friendships, and planning for the inevitable return of lengthened days and shortening time, and the stark return to reality which Spring will bring.

It will not be long before the wheel begins to turn again: the alarm switched off before it rings; the broken sleep punctuated by a forgotten ingredient unordered and the bed hopefully, sometimes, a welcome sanctuary of solid escape.

Our huge and honoured reward, though, is to be allowed to enjoy and live in this most spectacular and wondrous place.

Above Pope's Hole, winter light

Colin Daly stubble-burning above Higher Town

In the recipe section that follows, an orange band above the recipe implies that it is one from the Seven Stones pub, while a green band identifies a Bakery recipe.

For American weights, measures and oven temperatures see pp. 169, 171 and 187.

Bakery Guide

Whenever basic breads are made at St Martin's Bakery, we employ a yeast starter or 'poolish' to begin the fermentation process which raises the dough. This method of starting the yeast on its hungry quest several hours before introducing it to the flour adds a tangy flavour and chewiness to the bread and is not dissimilar to some sourdough methods. It also produces an even and dramatic rise in the end-product, and will create bread that will keep for several days or more, unlike those of quickly-risen doughs.

Normally, the sudden shock of introducing a small quantity of yeast to a bulk of flour, sugar, salt, fat and water can have an inhibiting effect on the yeast's performance and cause an irregularity in the rising and thus the growing size of the dough. For this reason we prepare a poolish some hours before we bake. This wakens the yeast from its dormant state and allow it to begin its reproductive cycle of breeding each and every twenty minutes! It is this generation of a huge colony of yeast which produces the bubbling of gasses, trapped in the dough, which will expand in the oven to create a large light loaf. The other by-product of this special yeast breeding is alcohol, which gives the bread a tangy flavour and fantastic keeping qualities.

Bubble, bubble: fermenting poolish

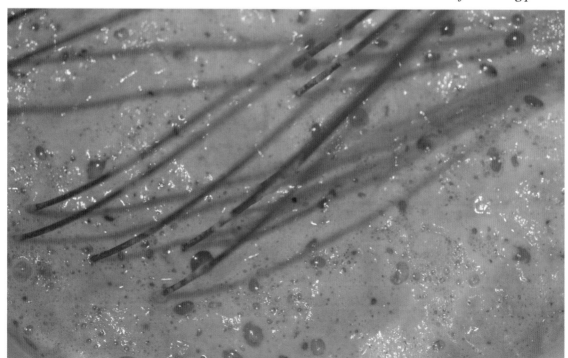

THE ISLAND INGREDIENT

enough for up to 10 loaves, or 50 rolls · use white or brown flour; rye gives a particularly good flavour

POOLISH

> 1.1 litres (2 pints) *lukewarm* water (more needed before using in bread)
> 1 teaspoon of sugar (optional)
> A large handful of flour
> 125g (4½ oz) fresh yeast or 2 packets dried yeast

1) Mix all of the above ingredients together with a whisk, cover and leave for at least three hours before using.

2) When you are ready to make the bread, the mixture needs to be diluted with 2.25 litres (4 pints) lukewarm water and added to 4.5 kg (9 lb 12 oz) flour. If you do not wish to use such large quantities you can refrigerate the remainder, so long as it is fed a small handful of flour twice a week to keep it alive. When it is finally removed from the fridge, add a little warm water along with the handful of flour to wake it up from its cool dormant state.

Fresh yeast can normally be obtained from your local baker or health food shop. Occasionally you may find a supermarket with an inhouse bakery that will actually give you some!

Once you have made your poolish starter, the next stage is to make beautifully-risen loaves with a good crust and a delicious white fluffy interior—loaves that will last a week if you can resist leaving them alone!

One large loaf

700g (1½ lb) strong white flour
About half this weight of poolish,
    —enough to form a silky,
    soft but not sticky, dough
1 tsp sugar
2 tsp salt
Plus, to use as you will:
Beaten egg for glaze
Knob of butter
Poppy/sesame/sunflower seeds for
decoration

Cut dough, reading for baking as rolls

BASIC LOAF

1) Dissolve the poolish in lukewarm water and whisk thoroughly.
2) The flour should then have the salt, sugar and fat added, and these ingredients rubbed in thoroughly.
3) The dissolved poolish is now added into a well made in the middle of the flour, and the flour gradually drawn into the poolish in the middle in a circular motion. This helps to 'wind up' the gluten in the flour to give you a big push at the baking stage, as the energies of the gluten are unleashed.
4) When your flour has been mixed thoroughly with the liquid it must be worked into a smooth elastic dough. This is tiring on the wrists but essential for a big rise.
5) The dough is then put in a cling-filmed bowl in a warm place where it will create its own moist warm environment and begin to rise. After a couple of hours, perhaps less in a warm humid kitchen, it will have doubled in size.
6) Again we attack it: kneading and and 'knocking it back'—deflating many of the gasses, responsible for its inflation, generated by the hungrily reproducing yeast cells. The more kneading, the bigger the rise you will later enjoy.
7) We now allow the dough to rise again till doubled in size, and once again

knock it back, working it well to exercise the gluten.

8) Divide dough into loaves if you made enough for several—approximately 1 kg of dough per large loaf.

9) You can bake them in greased bread tins or shape into bloomers. Rolls can be made by rolling the dough into a long sausage and cutting lumps which will fit into your palm. These are then rolled firmly on the table. Do not be tempted to strew flour around as the dough for the rolls will not grip the table, but rather allow you to create a firmly-rolled shape.

10) The rolls or loaves are left to rise again. Bread in tins should be allowed to rise just level with the top of the tin. Rolls are left until they are fifty per cent larger than when they started, and spongy when probed with a finger.

11) We then glaze the loaves or rolls with beaten egg and decorate with seeds. For rolls, we then slash the dough with a serrated knife or razor blade.

12) Bake at 200–220°C: 35 min. for loaves, 20 min. for rolls.

NOTES: Water from certain authorities contains levels of chlorine enough to inhibit your yeast's reproduction. Bottled water can be used as an alternative if you are concerned about this.
Our ovens are set at 220°C for breadbaking. There is a 'draw-down' effect on putting the bread in to cook, so the actual cooking is mainly around 200°C.

RUSSIAN BLACK BREAD

An unusual but delicious loaf which we have incorporated into our Bakery Holiday Courses to teach people a differently-flavoured loaf. Many years ago I experimented with Swedish flatbreads, which also contain ginger and the zest of an orange. The orange goes beautifully with the black treacle, rye flour and ginger in the following recipe. The taste and consistency of this loaf is somewhat similar to malt loaves and goes beautifully with soft cheeses.

one loaf · set-aside time, allow several hours

THE POOLISH STARTER	THE DOUGH MIXTURE
A handful of rye flour	200g (7 oz) rye flour
250 ml (9 fl oz) tepid water	200g (7 oz) wholemeal flour
25g (1 oz) fresh yeast	2 tsp salt
1 tsp caraway seeds	1 tsp sugar
1 tsp sugar	½ tsp ground ginger
	4 tbsps black treacle
	Zest of 1 orange
	Egg for glazing
	Seeds to decorate, if wished

1) Mix the poolish: the rye flour, tepid water, sugar and caraway seeds. Cream in the yeast and leave for an hour or so.

2) When working well add the black treacle to the poolish.

3) Mix all of the dry ingredients in the main mix together, including the orange zest. Add the now-frothy starter and mix to form a smooth but slightly wet dough. Some more water may needed to achieve this consistency. This is inevitably a messy process but rye will not stick to wet hands so once you have a dough it will help if you work it with clean wet hands.

4) Cover in a cling-filmed bowl and leave until doubled, about two hours, then knock back again, with wet hands and form a round ball.

5) Glaze with egg and if preferred cover with rye seeds, oats, or cracked wheat. Slash a cross in the top to open up the loaf, as rye has a tendency to split when cooking.

6) Now set aside somewhere warm to prove for another 45 min.

7) Bake at 200–220°C for 30–35 min. A little ball of the dough can be reserved to be added to the next black bread starter to give a really tangy taste.

PAIN DE CAMPAGNE

A heavy French country bread. It is developed by refreshing your starter each day to build up a colony of wild yeasts which will raise the dough with its gasses and finally produce a leavened bread when baked. This slow creation of the loaf will produce a specially chewy texture and a loaf which will last for days. It will have that unmistakable tangy Pain De Campagne *flavour and is delicious with sharp cheeses.*
For a picture, see p. 85.

For a picture, see p. 85.

makes four smallish loaves · needs to be started one week ahead

A handful of flour each day, over 7 days
I tsp honey each day
Water

1) Take a handful of the flour of your choice and add to this a little water to create a dough. Set aside in a container covered over with a damp cloth.

2) The following day, break down this dough by adding half a cup of water to which a teaspoonful of honey has been added, and pulling and squeezing the dough to take up the water. Next, add flour gradually and work until you again have a smooth dough. Once again set aside, loosely covered, to allow the wild yeasts access to your mix.

3) Repeat this every day for about a week. You will notice that the dough begins to rise more and more and begins to develop a network of gluten strands, demonstrating that the yeasts are really working hard.

4) The final day, after giving the dough its last refreshment, divide it equally in quarters and place in bannetons* to give some support during the final proving. These small loaves will prove more easily than two large ones.

5) When it has risen gently invert the dough onto a baking tray and slash with a noughts and crosses pattern. Place in an oven at 200–220°C and bake for 25–30 minutes.

*A banneton is a special rising basket made from cane, common in Southern Germany and France. Cane is the only material capable of providing the necessary moisture exchange during the fermentation process at the same time as ensuring the necessary oxygen supply. A heavily-floured tea towel in a large fruit bowl will however provide a satisfactory alternative.

ROSEMARY CIABATTA

Ciabatta means slipper or soft shoe in Italian. This is because of the flat shape of the bread and the soft cake-like consistency, derived from the olive oil, the milk, and the exceptionally wet nature of the dough. This is definitely a sticky-handed job!

We always retain dough from one day's baking to be added to the following day's, to create extra tanginess. This is not essential for this recipe, but if you wish to create some old dough simply mix a handful of flour with a pinch of sugar and a speck of yeast and bind with some water into a dough. This can be left covered overnight to develop a yeast colony and further develop the flavour of the bread.

The rosemary sprigs are optional so long as you change the name!

This ciabatta is delicious with a cheese like dolcelatte, or dipped into a bagna calda of warm butter, garlic, anchovy and pepper sauce. Make the experience complete with some Pinot Grigio!

makes one loaf · only the optional old dough is made previously

THE POOLISH STARTER

Some old dough (if available)
20g (¾–1 oz) fresh yeast
200ml (7 fl oz) water
A splash of milk
1 teaspoon sugar
Rosemary sprigs (optional)

THE DOUGH

300g (11 oz) white bread flour
1 teaspoon salt
1 tablespoon olive oil
Sun-dried tomatoes (optional)

1) Break down the old dough, if used, with the water, yeast and milk, squashing it in the hands to incorporate fully. Add the rosemary and a handful of flour. Leave for one hour.

2) Mix the poolish into the flour, salt, sun-dried tomatoes if used, and olive oil, using a winding motion to strengthen and elongate the gluten. The more winding, the easier the dough will be, the more malleable.

3) Set aside to prove in a covered bowl for about an hour and once risen again work the dough with more winding and kneading.

4) Pour the dough onto a flour-dusted baking sheet, tucking the edges under with heavily-floured fingers, into a 30 cm (12-in) oval shape. Drizzle with more olive oil and decorate with chopped rosemary or flour to give that 'leopard loaf' look.

5) Bake at 200–220°C for 25–30 min. Tap the bottom for that hollow sound to indicate the loaf is cooked throughout. Cool on a wire rack.

For a guide to US measures, see pp 169, 171 and 187.

PUMPERNICKEL

Pumpernickel is another non-yeasted bread, insofar as no cultured yeast is added. The rise in the loaf is due to the invasion of natural yeasts surrounding us all of the time. Pumpernickel is a delicious bread expressly made to be eaten with hams, garlic sausages, smoked cheeses and salamis, and as such should be sliced very thinly. It will keep for a long time in the refrigerator. Its name is said to be derived from a German phrase for 'Devil's wind'. Baker, beware!

makes two loaves   ·   needs two to three days to rise

600g (1lb 5 oz) wholemeal flour (coarse if possible)
600g (1lb 5 oz) rye flour (coarse dark rye if possible)
200g (7 oz) barley flour (or more wholemeal if barley not available)
1 tsp each of these:
    ground coriander, ground cumin, caraway seeds and fennel seeds
1 good handful whole or split wheat
1 handful of rolled oats
2 tsp salt
2 tablespoons of honey
1 large tbsp black treacle

1)   Mix all of the dry ingredients together in a bowl, adding the water to make a smooth dough. Rye flour is very sticky to work with, so a scrupulously clean table and hands from the start are essential. It is also a good idea to work with wetted hands as this prevents rye from sticking too much.

2)   Add water to make a moist dough, next adding the honey and black treacle and work this through the dough.

3)   Press the dough as firmly and flatly as possible into a bread tin. A wet spatula is good for this. If you wish, you can sprinkle some wheat, cumin seeds or caraway seeds on the top and press them in.

4)   Cover with cling film and put in a warm place for three days, until the natural yeasts will have caused a very slight raising of the dough. The proof of the yeast working is a sponginess to the dough when pressed.

5)   The bread in the tins is now placed on a griddle under which water has been poured so that the bread will steam-cook. The whole tray is then covered with tin foil to keep the steam in (making sure the foil will not

come into contact with the dough while it is cooking) and baked slowly at 110°C for 4½ hours.

6) Finally, remove the foil, carefully tip the steaming loaves out of the tins, turn up the oven to 175°C and bake for a further 20 min. to firm the loaf up. Cool on a wire rack.

Barney kneads the Lawrence Loaf

THE LAWRENCE LOAF

The Lawrence Loaf is mentioned on page 24 and pictured in the making above, but it is truly a flavoured version of a conventional loaf rather than a different bread in itself.

1) We take 1kg of standard bread dough (see p. 74), mix in two handfuls of dried sea lettuce, one handful of sun-dried tomatoes and the same of cubed feta cheese.

2) The dough is then formed into a bloomer shape, glazed with beaten egg, dusted with flour, slashed with a razor blade for decoration, and baked for 30 min. at 200°C.

IRISH SODA BREAD

Soda bread is a non-yeasted bread which is risen by the gasses created when an acid and an alkali are mixed together, namely cream of tartar and bicarbonate of soda.

In my many travels to Eire, the home of this bread, I have tried without success to obtain good soda bread flour. It seems that as in England many of the smaller mills and bakeries have been replaced with huge milling and baking conglomerates. In this recipe, then, I have tried to replicate the soft rustic flours that may have been available in times long past.

We normally mix white and brown flour 50:50 for this in the Bakery.

We find it difficult to obtain buttermilk on any regular basis so I always keep some soured milk to add to the water to give more flavour and the lactic acid needed to ensure a good rise.

Serve for preference with a soup or stew—and a glass of Guinness, of course! In Ireland, the deep cutting of the cross in the bread is said to 'let the devil out'!

makes one loaf

450g (1 lb) white and wholemeal flour, combined 50:50
A handful of rolled oats
½ tsp salt
¼ tsp bicarbonate of soda
¼ tsp cream of tartar
Large knob of butter
¼ tsp baking powder (to guarantee a big rise)
Buttermilk, or soured milk and water
Egg for glazing

My father, also called Toby, but christened John, died twenty-eight years ago and sadly never saw the fruition of St Martin's Bakery. It was only through reading Elizabeth David's ENGLISH BREAD AND YEAST COOKERY in the terror of the early days that I discovered that the finest soda bread flour was milled by the monks of St Joseph's Monastery, Roscrae, County Tipperary, the school at which my father was educated.

1) Mix together the flour, oats and salt in a bowl. Work in the knob of butter; this helps keep the crumb of the bread soft and moist.

2) In a separate container, mix together the cream of tartar, bicarbonate of soda and baking powder and add them to the flour mixture along with the salt.

3) Add the buttermilk/soured milk and water to the flour to create a moist dough.

4) As soon as they are moistened, the raising agents will begin reacting and giving off their gasses, so we do not leave this to rise like conventional bread. Roll the dough into a rough ball and glaze with the egg. Liberally sprinkle with flour. With a serrated knife, saw a cross in the loaf almost through to the bottom to create the distinctive farls.

5) Without wasting any time, bake in a hot oven, 200–220°C, for about 35 min. Cool on a wire rack.

Back left: apple sourdough. right: irish soda. foreground: pain de campagne

APPLE SOURDOUGH

This is a sourdough process bread which is risen by the capture and manipulation of wild yeasts that surround us constantly. The starter is left for one week to ferment and develop a rich yeast culture which is then educated to make bread rather than cider!

Literally any fruit or vegetable which will ferment and create a wild yeast starter can be tried. Different ones I have used have been artichoke, parsnip and pear. Sourdough is fabulous with strong cheeses.

makes three loaves · preparations ten days in advance

3 cooking apples, peeled (1 used at the start, 2 later)
1 tbsp caster sugar
Strong white flour
   (worked in over three days, enough to form a dough each time)
2 handfuls rye flour
3 tsp honey
1 large knob butter
Water and salt

1) Chop one apple into chunks and add the sugar, plus water to just cover the apple. Set aside for one week, uncovered, stirring occasionally. This starter will be invaded by wild yeasts and begin to ferment.

2) Mash this starter with half a cup of water and a teaspoon of honey, and then work in white flour until a dough is achieved. Set aside somewhere warm.

3) The next day, mash this dough again with a half cup of water and a spoon of honey, once again working in white flour until a soft dough is achieved.

4) The third day, mash again to 'let down' the dough with another water and honey mixture. Now add a couple of handfuls of rye flour, two teaspoons of salt and more white flour until a firm dough is achieved.

5) Sauté gently the other two peeled and cubed apples with a large knob of butter, and when well cooled disperse carefully into the dough.

6) Shape into three loaves and leave for a couple of hours to prove and rise by about fifty per cent. Glaze with beaten egg, slash to educate the loaves where to split (see the loaves in the picture on p. 85) and bake on an oven tray at 200–220°C for 25–30 min., or until a hollow sound is heard when tapping the bottom of the cooked loaves.

Soups and Stocks from Bakery and Seven Stones

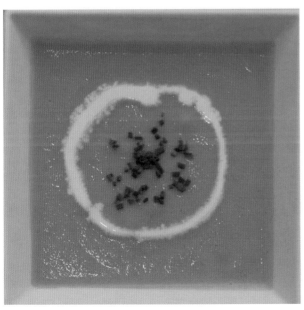

VEGETABLE STOCK

This delicious stock is used as a starter for many of our soups, our vegetarian risottos and other dishes. The rule with stocks is not to throw in every odd remnant because it's there, but to make a good blend. This recipe uses some particularly tasty vegetables; we do, of course, vary what we use according to season and day-to-day choice. Lemon juice, a teaspoon of honey, or white wine can be added for extra sweetness.

2 large onions, chopped with the skin still on
2 cloves garlic
225g (8 oz) carrots
1 stick celery
½ bulb fennel
1 sweet potato, diced
50g (2 oz) unsalted butter
A handful of parsley
1 sprig of rosemary
1 bayleaf
A good twist or two of black pepper

1) Chop the vegetables into small pieces.
2) Sauté the onion, garlic, carrots, celery, fennel and sweet potato in the butter until soft.
3) Add three pints of water, the rosemary sprig, the parsley, a bayleaf and a good twist or two of black pepper.
4) Next pour in three pints of cold water, bring to the boil and reduce by half.
5) Strain and use, or refrigerate/freeze for later dishes.

FISH STOCK

With the daily deliveries of local fish here at the Seven Stones, we are often full to the gunnels with fish frames of every description. However, these are not wasted, and are used to create the supremely delicate sauces that accompany our varied fish menu.
The turbot, brill and sole bones we are left with after the travails of Ian Mitchell and Joel and Martin Bond produce the best stocks, but any fish frames can be made to produce a beautiful stock.

1 kg (2 lb 4 oz) fish frames
50g (2 oz) unsalted butter
1 onion, sliced with the skin on
1 leek, sliced thinly
1 carrot, sliced thinly
¼ bulb fennel, finely sliced
    or a sprig of wild fennel, or some fennel seeds, ground
1 bunch fresh dill, or 1 tbsp dried dill
A glass of white wine
A handful of chopped parsley
A good twist or two of black pepper
A squeeze of lemon

1)   Sauté the onion, leek, carrots and fennel in the butter, until soft.
2)   Add the fish frames and cook, stirring for 5 to 10 min., or until the fish flesh left on the frames begins to cook and fall away.
3)   Shoot in the white wine and bubble until it is almost evaporated.
4)   Next, add the chopped parsley, the dill, pepper and about 2 litres (4 pints) of cold water.
5)   Bring to the boil and simmer gently for about an hour.
6)   Sieve to remove bones and vegetables. Add a squeeze of lemon and stir in.
7)   Use, or store in the refrigerator or freezer for later.

BEEF STOCK

1 kg (2 lb 4 oz) veal/beef bones,
    plus some trimmings if you have a kind butcher
3 large onions, skin on
3 washed carrots
3 sticks of celery
1 sweet potato
1 leek
4 cloves of garlic
1 large sprig of rosemary
2 tomatoes
2 bayleaves
2 whole cloves
A good twist of black pepper

1) Put the beef bones on a large roasting tray and bake in a hot oven for 30 min.
2) Roughly chop the onions (with skin on), the carrots, celery, sweet potato (skin on), leek and garlic and add these to the beef bones and roast for another 20 min.
3) Remove from the oven and add to a large stockpot. Place in the chopped tomatoes, the rosemary, bayleaves, whole cloves and black pepper.
4) Add around 4½ litres (8 pints) of water and bring to the boil. Bubble gently for four to six hours, skimming any unwanted matter from the top. Strain and refrigerate.
5) Allow to cool and remove any set fat on the surface. This stock is ready to be used or can be frozen and defrosted as you need.

CHICKEN STOCK

1 whole chicken
 or waste cuts (wings, bones, trimmings and skin) from your butcher
2 large onions, roughly chopped, skin on
2 cloves garlic
1 stick of celery
3 carrots, finely chopped
1 sprig of rosemary
1 handful of parsley
1 bayleaf
50g (2 oz) unsalted butter
1 glass white wine
A good twist of pepper

1) Fry the onion, garlic, chopped carrots and chopped celery in the butter until softened. Add the chicken pieces and continue to fry for a few minutes. Pour in the white wine and enjoy the aromas. Next add the bayleaf, the parsley, stalks included, and a good twist or two of black pepper.
2) Add 2½ litres (5 pints) of water and simmer for 2–3 hours, skimming the surface. Strain and refrigerate.
3) When cooled, remove the set fat. Use or freeze for later addition.

Stocks are very important to us at the Seven Stones. The approach is similar each time with the stock made and a slow period of reduction employed to concentrate and enrich the flavours to be enjoyed in our final dishes.

HONEY PARSNIP SOUP

800g (1 lb 12 oz) celeriac, to cubes of about 1 cm
200g (7 oz) onion, finely chopped
2 cloves of garlic, finely chopped
100g (3½ oz) butter
About 4 sprigs of thyme and 1 bayleaf
100 ml (3½ fl oz) double cream
1 litre (1¾ pints) chicken or vegetable stock

1) Sweat the onion and the garlic in the butter for 4 min.
2) Add the diced celeriac and a pinch of salt and pepper, and sweat under a lid very slowly for 8 min. Be careful not to colour the celeriac. Add the thyme and bayleaf, and continue sweating for another 8–10 min., or until very soft.
3) Add the vegetable or chicken stock and continue to cook slowly until the celeriac has completely broken down.
4) Remove the thyme and garlic and purée in a liquidiser or food processor, adding the cream until smooth.
5) Adjust the seasoning and pass through a conical strainer if you have one.

CELERIAC SOUP

800g (1 lb 12 oz) parsnips, peeled and diced
150g (5 oz) butter
200g (7 oz) sliced onion
3 cloves of garlic, crushed
1200ml (2¼ pints) chicken or vegetable stock
100ml (3½ fl oz) double cream
2 tbsp honey
Seasoning

1) Melt the butter in a heavy-bottomed saucepan. Sweat the onion and garlic for 5 min.
2) Add the diced parsnips, and still on a low heat cook, stirring occasionally, for 15 min.—until the parsnips are coloured a little, but not a lot.
3) Now add the stock. Bring to the boil and then turn down to a simmer. Cook until the parsnip is soft.
4) Now in a food processor or liquidiser blend the soup until smooth, adding the cream and honey to taste. Check the seasoning.

This is a regular on the Seven Stones menu. Nothing better than a bowl of warming soup on a cool autumn's evening. The soup has a great colour and is a bit of a different spin on the usual carrot soup.

As you can see in the pictures here and on the opening page to this section (p. 87) I have garnished the soup with some chopped chives, double cream, and syrup from the stem ginger jar.

Serve with a hot crusty roll, sit by the fire and enjoy.

serves 4

750g (1 lb 10 oz) carrots,
   peeled and roughly diced
250g (9 oz) sliced onion
1 clove of crushed garlic
150g (5 oz) butter
1 tsp honey
Juice of ½ a lemon
½ a preserved stem ginger
1 litre (1¾ pints) vegetable or
chicken stock, or water

1)   Heat a heavy-based saucepan. Melt the butter and sweat the onions and garlic until soft but with no colour.

2)   Add the diced carrots and sweat for a further 5 min., then add the honey. Stir and coat the carrots with the honey, then add the water/stock.

3)   Once the carrots are almost cooked, add the chopped ginger and cook out for a further 10 min.

4)   Remove the soup from the heat, then blend the soup in a liquidiser and pass through a sieve.

5)   Now you can finish the soup. Taste it, add a little lemon juice if you wish, maybe a splash of cream if you like creamier soups; or if the ginger flavour isn't strong enough, add a little of the syrup from the ginger jar, and of course check the seasoning!

6)   Garnish with chopped chives or parsley (or as in the note above).

This Seven Stones favourite is the simplest of soups when all types of squashes are coming into season, and has a beautifully sweet and rounded flavour. We save all of the trimmings and add other vegetable and herbs to make a vegetable stock to be used if the dish is to be enjoyed by vegetarians and indeed it wholeheartedly is !

serves 6

500g (1 lb 2 oz) sweet potato, peeled and diced
500g (1 lb 2 oz) butternut squash, peeled, deseeded and diced
200g (7 oz) onion, sliced
3 cloves of garlic, crushed
1 litre (1¾ pints) vegetable/chicken stock
Fresh nutmeg

1) Heat a heavy-bottomed sauce pan, melt the butter and sweat the onion and garlic for 5 min. but with no colour.
2) Now add the butternut. Season a little and sweat for another 5–10 min., until the butternut starts to break down.
3) Add the sweet potato with a few gratings of fresh nutmeg, and stir in. Then add the water/stock.
4) Cook the soup for about 20 min. until the potato is soft. Remove from heat, liquidise and pass through a sieve.
5) Again at this point, you can add cream, or whisk in a little butter, and add more nutmeg if needed—but always remember to check the seasoning.
6) A decoration with chopped chives can be used.

ST MARTIN'S *BOUILLABAISSE*

Bouillabaisse *is more of a mixed fish stew than a soup, its golden colour being created by the addition of saffron and tomato purée. With its origins on the Mediterranean coasts of France, this dish is a reflection of the many varieties of fish that are found there.*

The regional slants on bouillabaisse are hotly contested, and so it is with a degree of cheek that we appropriate this recipe to St Martin's and offer our local variation. The fish ingredient choice is yours to experiment with. However, there are a few basic rules to follow to make a good bouillabaisse, which are the addition of olive oil and saffron, and the good reduction to concentrate the flavours and create a stew-like consistency. During the season we have a huge variety of mixed fish landing at our door so the bouillabaisse varies with the fishermen's catch. The varieties we use are:

- *Red mullet*
- *Grey mullet*
- *Gurnard*
- *White fish such as cod or hake*
- *Monkfish*
- *John Dory*
- *Shellfish such as lobster, crawfish or langoustines cut lengthways. Mussels in their shells are a good substitute.*

The varieties of this dish are endless and colour can be added by using fish such as salmon, although it is not a Mediterranean fish.

for 6 to 8 people. Allow about 225g (8 oz) of fish per person.

Up to 2 kg (4.4 lbs) fish
4 cloves garlic, chopped
2 onions, chopped
I bulb fennel
4 tomatoes, deseeded and chopped
I tbsp tomato purée
225g (½ lb) new potatoes, thinly sliced in the round
I teaspoon saffron
I bayleaf

6 tbsp extra virgin olive oil
Large glass of white wine
2.2 litres (4 pints) fish/vegetable stock (see p. 88)
Spinach/sea spinach for taste and a deep green colour contrast
Good organic bread for dipping or for garlic croutons
A good amount of seasoning

1) Heat the oil in a heavy pan and sweat the chopped fennel, onion, tomatoes, and garlic until soft.
2) Add the bayleaf, tomato purée and saffron. Pour in the white wine and sizzle for a minute or so.
3) Add the stock and some seasoning and bring to a gentle boil.
4) Next, add the thinly-sliced potatoes and continue to cook for 10 more minutes.
5) Begin to add the fish, the firmer ones first (monkfish, gurnard and mullet). All of the fish must be in nice large chunks to hold their shape. Add any shellfish you have, and finally the white fish and roughly-torn spinach.
6) Boil well to reduce to a stew-like consistency. Remember to taste for seasoning as this dish will take plenty of pepper and some salt for flavouring.
7) Serve with good bread for soaking up the liquid. A spoonful of aïoli (see page 108) can be added to the top of each served bowl and a sprinkling of parsley or fresh dill for decoration.

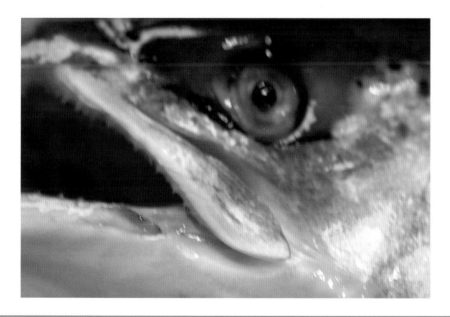

For a guide to US measures, see pp 169, 171 and 187.

BURGUNDY CRAB BISQUE

Among the soups that we make at the Bakery this is in my opinion the ultimate! The title describes the russet-red colour the soup takes on after its aromatic reduction.

This recipe may be a little difficult to quantify, because Mark Pender, our crab supplier, brings us the picked-out shells and bodies in the early morning along with his fantastic white and brown crab meat, in return for a pasty that he takes to sea that day for his lunch. Sometimes we have up to half a carrier bag of picked claws and bodies, and sometimes less. But our approach is always the same, although the soup has many different identities and flavours relying on the proportion of crab shells and bodies to claws.

This bisque improves massively after two or three days of reboiling and reducing. Nothing more is required except good bread and a glass of Burgundy.

feeds 6 to 8, depending upon the quantity of meat on the crabs

Two large cooked crabs
Fresh or dried dill, leaving some for decoration
125g (4 oz) butter (to sauté the vegetables)
One Spanish (large) onion with its skin still on
1 leek (optional)
Two cloves garlic, crushed
A handful of cut sweet peppers
400g (14 oz) can of organic chopped tomatoes
2 tbsp tomato purée
Fennel frond or ¼ bulb
Large glass (250 ml) red wine
Juice of one lemon
Double cream for decoration
Seasoning

1) Pick out the claws and the liver from the main shell and leave them to be added to the finished sieved soup.
2) The pieces of picked out shell are drizzled with olive oil and fresh dill, and

we then bake them in a hot oven, 200–220°C, for 20–30 min. (remember to pick out the gills attached to the main body, nicknamed 'dead man's fingers', and obvious from the description).

3) When these are retrieved from the oven, we then pound the hot shells with the end of a rolling pin into small fragments, in a large pan.

4) In a separate large pan and in the butter, sauté off the garlic with all of the onion (skin on and very roughly chopped), adding one leek if you have one and a handful of chopped sweet peppers, until soft.

5) Add the organic tomatoes, tomato purée and a large glass of ordinary red wine (save the Burgundy itself to drink later!), and around 2.2 litres (4 pints) water, along with a sprig of fennel leaves, or ¼ of a fennel bulb, again roughly chopped.

6) Season with lemon juice, sea salt and lots of ground pepper, and add four pints of water. Bubble on the stove and add the roasted crab shells.

7) Go on bubbling fiercely and let it reduce for about an hour.

8) Strain through a colander to allow the small fragments of crab meat to remain in the finished soup. while removing the shells.

9) Finish with a splash of double cream and some fresh or dried dill.

"Half way through the 2004 season, my second at St Martin's Hotel, I believe I truly got over my car crash. It nearly wasn't like that! Coming back to Scilly was make or break for me as a chef. I was still not sure I even wanted to stay within the profession.

"Brad and Natalie, two great friends with whom I had worked on St Martin's in 2002, were back that season too. It helped. It was great to be back on the island, seeing all the faces I'd known. I felt I had come home. Yet 2004 was a tough season for me, running the larder section at the age of nineteen. My demi-chef was twenty-eight, and my commis-chef was thirty-one. Moreover, they were a married couple. Rupert and Sheona came to be friends of mine, in spite of the difficulty of the situation, and we'd later meet up in Melbourne, Australia, in 2005, after they emigrated there.

"The hotel was always busy that season. Unlike the hotel of today, where there is both a bistro and a restaurant, we only had the one restaurant and the one kitchen. There was bar food at lunchtime downstairs in the Round Island Bar, the food coming from the larder section in the upstairs kitchen. For the busy months in the summer, we employed another commis, Ross, who was to help out at lunchtimes on the larder. Yet one week into being there Ross broke his ankle, falling off the back of a quad bike on a quest to fish for grey mullet with his teeth. Nine weeks later the cast came off at last, which was a great help.

"Yet in the midst all this hard work, I realised something had changed. I had stopped feeling everyone owed me something, and knew I had to get out there and do it. I got the love back for the job. Stew Eddy was just happy to have me back for my Yorkshire puddings for the staff Sunday roast! And towards the end of the season I decided all I needed was a holiday—a big one.

"As I played with ideas of going to Costa Rica or Sri Lanka with Ross on a surfing trip, my friend Brad, from the hotel, invited me to go travelling with him and Natalie. Brad and I went on a 'bloke's holiday' for a month in Thailand before travelling on to Australia and meeting up with Natalie ready to buy a car and travel round Australia. Just as much as St Martin's had healed me, these places and the cuisines I discovered were going to change my whole career."

PAULIE WEBSDALE

Salad Dressings, Sauces, Oils and Ingredients

By the time spring comes, the Seven Stones herb garden is abundant with a huge variety of herbs and salads, providing us with a verdant selection of fresh produce to accompany our dishes. Most of our dishes leave the kitchen alongside salads or salad garnishes to finish the plate and to add a light balance to some of the more complex dishes. The herbs are used both in the cooking processes in the kitchen and in the production of the many varied salad dressings we employ. So, since we're proud of the variety we offer, here is a whole section on dressings and sauces.

dresses salad for 10 servings

We produce large quantities of a basic vinaigrette dressing which is for general use in the kitchen and provides a base for the production of alternatively-flavoured herb dressings. This basic vinaigrette is kept sealed and refrigerated and is constantly replenished as it is used, producing a base dressing that intensifies and matures like a fine wine. Each time it is used, the container is vigorously shaken to re-emulsify and mix the dressing, as it will separate out in the fridge.

1 tbsp balsamic or red wine vinegar
1 tsp sea salt
2 tsp lemon juice
2 cloves garlic, crushed and ground to a paste on the chopping board
1 tsp Dijon mustard
5 tbsp extra virgin, first-pressed, olive oil
A couple of twists of black pepper

1)   In a large bowl, whisk the lemon juice, salt, balsamic or red wine vinegar and garlic paste together until the salt is dissolved as it will not dissolve when the oil is added.

2)   Incorporate the Dijon mustard, mixing in thoroughly. Then gradually add the olive oil, dribble by dribble, whisking well to emulsify and mix to a smooth consistency. Crack in a couple of twists of black pepper and allow the dressing to stand while your salad is assembled. Or refrigerate for later use, as it is or as a basis for herb dressings.

3)   Once you have this base dressing the choice of herb additions is yours.

One metre beyond the kitchen door we have a fine rosemary bush which is used profusely. To make a rosemary dressing, we simply pound a couple of sprigs of leaves in a mortar with a pestle and add them to the base dressing, allowing them to infuse for a while before straining the mix. Other herb dressings we use are tarragon, basil, dill, marjoram and coriander. The method is the same for each one and they can remain in your fridge labelled and ready.

HERB OIL

make a supply to last, according to taste

A method of creating rosemary-infused oil for cooking is to place three or four whole sprigs of rosemary in a wine bottle. Fill with olive oil and stand the bottle on a sunny shelf for a couple of weeks. This oil is fantastic for cooking lamb and making Bolognese sauce.

Other oils can give distinctive flavour to dressings—three we use are avocado, sesame and walnut. All are fantastic in combination with mizuna and nutty-tasting rocket. These are only used in half-teaspoonfuls, to give a hint of nuttiness—be sparing, lest the dressings overpower the flavours of your mixed salads. In mid to late summer we also have a bountiful crop of raspberries. One handful of these plump berries can be crushed and added to your dressing for a sweeter flavour. If you're unlucky enough not to have access to fresh raspberries, a couple of tablespoons of raspberry vinegar in place of the balsamic/red wine vinegar will give a splendid result. Don't be afraid to experiment. Once you have emulsified your oils and vinegars and seasoned, the arena is yours. Any flavour of herb oil is easy to make: just follow these steps.

1) Blanch the herb in boiling water then quickly refresh in iced water.
2) Dry out the herb in a tea towel, then blend with olive oil. Either pass the oil through a fine sieve at this point or use just as it is.

REDUCED BALSAMIC DRESSING

Here is a recipe to make your own thick balsamic, from the cheap stuff. It will save you having to locate one of the reduced balsamic dressings, although they are becoming common in most supermarkets. We use this one for the Goldeneye Mullet recipe on page 128.

120ml (4 fl oz) cheap balsamic vinegar
60ml (2 fl oz) ruby port
120ml (4 fl oz) apple juice

1) Place all the ingredients into a small sauce pan, bring to the boil, and then turn down to a simmer. Watch you do not burn the dressing when it starts to become thick. Leave to cool before using.

QUICK CREAMY DRESSING

30 ml (1 fl oz) cider vinegar
15g (1 tbsp) Dijon mustard
2 cloves garlic, finely chopped
4g (1 tsp) caster sugar
125 ml (4 fl oz) olive oil
125 ml (4 fl oz) crème fraîche
Seasoning, to taste

1) In a mixing bowl, combine the vinegar, mustard, sugar and garlic.
2) Slowly add the oil, incorporating it into the dressing as you do.
3) Lightly whip the crème fraîche, and whisk that too into the dressing.

ANCHOVY DRESSING

20g (3 fl oz) Dijon mustard
55g (1¾ oz) can of anchovy fillets, drained
1 clove garlic, finely chopped
60 ml (4 tbsp) lemon juice
100 ml (3½ fl oz) sunflower oil
125 ml (4 fl oz) olive oil
Seasoning, to taste

1) In a mixing bowl, crush up the garlic and add the anchovies. Mix with the Dijon mustard with the back of a fork until blended.
2) At this point, season quite generously with black pepper. Then, using a small whisk, blend in the lemon juice.
3) Slowly whisk in first the sunflower oil and then the olive oil.
4) Check the seasoning.

SIMPLE OIL AND LEMON DRESSING

This is the basic but very lively dressing used for the calamari salad on page 146. Combine the ingredients in a small jug.

100ml (4 fl oz) olive oil
35ml (2 tbsp) lemon juice and the zest of 1 lime
15ml (1 tbsp) water
Salt and pepper to taste

HONEY LIME DRESSING

Not to be confused with the citrus dressings below and overleaf, this is a rich sweet dressing with more than just citrus to offer!

15 ml (1 tbsp) lemon juice
15 ml (1 tbsp) lime juice
15 ml (1 tbsp) honey
45 ml (3 tbsp) olive oil
45 ml (3 tbsp) walnut oil
30g (1 oz) chopped chives
Seasoning, to taste

1)   In a mixing bowl, whisk together the lemon and lime juices and the honey.
2)   Now slowly add the olive oil, followed by the walnut oil.
3)   Mix in the chopped chives and season.

HAZELNUT DRESSING

15g (½ oz) Dijon mustard
30 ml (2 tbsp) white wine vinegar
1 clove garlic, finely chopped
1 tsp caster sugar
100 ml (3½ fl oz) hazelnut oil
20g (¾ oz) peeled chopped hazelnuts

1)   In a mixing bowl, whisk together the mustard, vinegar, garlic and sugar.
2)   Slowly incorporate the hazelnut oil, and then mix in the chopped nuts.

CITRUS DRESSING

This dressing plus hollandaise sauce are perfect with the turbot recipe (p. 148)

Rind and juice of 1 lemon, 1 orange, 1 lime and 1 grapefruit
50g (1¾ oz) caster sugar
50 ml (2 tbsp) water

1)   Peel each fruit and cut the skin into fine strips. Place in cold water, bring to the boil, then drain. Mix the water and sugar in a saucepan. Bring to the boil for 10 seconds and then turn down to a simmer. Add juice from fruits to the saucepan, adding the chopped skin. Reduce to a syrup and leave to cool.

DILL MUSTARD DRESSING

This is a very simple mix that goes excellently with salmon (see p. 136).

10 tbsp mayonnaise
1 tbsp honey
1 tbsp soy sauce
1 tsp smooth Dijon mustard
25g (1 oz) freshly-chopped dill

BÉCHAMEL SAUCE

This is a useful sauce if prepared properly and can form the basis of many other sauces. Grated parmesan, gruyère or blue cheese can be added at the final stage to make a cheese sauce. Chicken stock and cream can be added to make a cream sauce, parsley added to make a parsley sauce, and a reduced fish stock and chopped fresh dill added to make a sauce to complement fish dishes. Finely-chopped onion or shallot can be added at the foaming-butter stage for extra flavour.
The simple sauce is the classic for lasagne and is used in the recipe on p. 138.

600ml (1 pint) milk
60g (2 oz) butter
60g (2 oz) sieved plain or strong flour
¼ grated nutmeg
Bayleaf (optional)
Seasoning

1) Warm the milk to blood temperature in one saucepan. Add a bayleaf if desired; set aside and keep warm.
2) In a heavy-bottomed pan, melt the butter until foaming. Remove from the stove and add the flour, mixing thoroughly to a smooth paste.
3) Place back onto a gentle heat and gradually add and whisk in the warm milk. At first, you will have a paste consistency, but as you add the remainder of the milk it will loosen to a smooth sauce.
4) Add a few grates of nutmeg. Taste, season and continue to heat gently. Stir the bubbling mixture for ten minutes to remove any crude flour taste.
5) Set aside and keep warm. If you need to reheat, place the Béchamel pan inside a larger pan with hot water in it and stir constantly.

HOLLANDAISE SAUCE

1 tbsp white wine vinegar
1 tbsp water
3 egg yolks
200g (7 oz) clarified butter or ghee
    (this is pure butter which has all the milk and solids removed)
Juice of ½ a lemon
Salt and pepper

1)   In a bowl, mix the egg yolks, vinegar and water and over a pan of gently
      simmering water whisk until thick, leaving it foamy.
2)   Slowly add the clarified butter to the egg mixture until fully incorporated.
3)   Remove from heat and season with salt, pepper and lemon juice.

WHITE WINE SAUCE

Used for the chicken dish on p. 140.

1 onion
1 clove garlic
1 carrot
2 sticks of celery
1 chicken carcass
100ml (3½ fl oz) white wine
150ml (¼ pint) double cream
1 sprig of tarragon

1)   With the chicken carcass cut into small pieces and in a saucepan, add half
      the onion and the carrot and celery. Bring to the boil in 2 litres (3½ pints)
      of water, turn down to a simmer and leave for 2 hours. Then strain (retain
      the liquid but discard the carcass).
2)   In a separate saucepan fry off the other half of the onion and garlic in a little
      butter until soft, with no colour. Add wine and reduce by two thirds.
3)   Add chicken stock and reduce on the stove, down to approximately 250 ml
      (½ pint).
4)   Now add the double cream. Bring just to the boil, turn down and reduce
      to sauce consistency. In a liquidiser or blender add the tarragon. Blend, pass
      through a sieve, and season.

TARTARE SAUCE

This is perfect with the battered fish recipe on page 128.

2 egg yolks
1 tbsp Dijon mustard
25ml (2 tbsp) water
100ml sunflower oil
50g (2 oz) chopped capers
50g (2 oz) chopped gherkins
Juice of ½ a lemon
1 tbsp chopped parsley

1) Whisk the eggs, mustard and water until they are a unity: thick, creamy and pale yellow in colour.

2) Slowly add the sunflower oil, adding a little more water if mixture becomes too thick. Once mayonnaise is formed, add chopped gherkins and capers, lemon juice and parsley. Season to taste.

BÉARNAISE SAUCE

A delicious and light sauce that complements our mouthwatering Tresco beef beautifully.

5 tbsp (75ml) white wine
2 shallots, finely chopped
2 tbsp (30 ml) tarragon vinegar or white wine vinegar
   (add chopped tarragon at the end if you can't find tarragon vinegar)
175g (6 oz) salted butter
3 free-range egg yolks
A squeeze of lemon
A good amount of black pepper

1) Place the wine, the vinegar, the black pepper and the chopped shallots in a pan. Heat vigorously until reduced to about two tablespoons in volume. Place this in a double boiler in which the water is not in contact with the top pan.

3) Cube the butter, add to the reduced liquid and melt.

4) Beat the three egg yolks and then whisk into the melted butter and sauce reduction until a creamy consistency is arrived at.

5) Finally squeeze in some lemon juice, a few drops of water and some chopped tarragon leaves if you were unable to use tarragon vinegar.

THE ISLAND INGREDIENT

PESTO

Pesto's origins are north of the beautiful Tuscan countryside we visit each autumn—returning home with bags stuffed with olives, olive oil, balsamic vinegars, pine nuts, cured meats and huge lumps of parmigiano reggiano and pecorino cheeses, with which we make this versatile sauce.

It's a great accompaniment to many vegetable and meat recipes, and we also use it freely in pasta dishes combined with olives, feta cheese, and sundried tomatoes to create simple and quick vegetarian alternatives.

Thai basil gives a nuttier and more peppery taste. (We sometimes use rocket for the same reason.) If you can't find pecorino use double-quantity parmesan. Pesto will keep well in the fridge, although it must be vigorously shaken before use to amalgamate the ingredients.

for six good servings

100g (3½ oz) pine nuts
200 ml (7–8 fl oz) extra virgin olive oil
2 cloves of garlic, crushed to a paste
2 large bunches of basil
50g (2 oz) parmesan cheese
50g (2 oz) strong pecorino cheese (sharp sheep's cheese)

1) Lightly roast the pine nuts in the oven, 3–5 min., turning to prevent burning.
2) Put the olive oil, garlic paste and basil in a food processor and blend well.
3) Remove from the processor and finely grate in the cheeses.
4) Taste and season with salt and pepper.

SIMPLE SUN-BLUSHED TOMATOES

6 large fresh plum tomatoes
1 clove garlic, puréed
1 tbsp chopped thyme
1 tsp salt
8 whole black peppercorns
100ml (3½ oz) olive/vegetable oil

1) Mix all ingredients in a mixing bowl, and then lay them out on a baking tray. Place in oven at 100°C for 3 hours. If you want to keep rather than used them, you can now place them in a Kilner jar covered with oil.

AÏOLI (GARLIC MAYONNAISE)

This addictive dish is French by origin and is affectionately referred to as 'the butter of Provence'. Used as an accompaniment to many types of

food, it goes beautifully with poached eggs, potato dishes, fish cakes, calamari and fish'n'chips.

It is a simple dish to prepare but some patience is required, for if the olive oil is added too quickly the mix will split and curdle. If this happens, whisk an egg yolk separately and then add the split mixture gradually to the egg while whisking. Your aïoli will come back to a thick creamy texture again.

This aïoli will last refrigerated for 3 to 5 days, if you can resist eating it all in one, and will actually improve with keeping.

It's fantastic mixed into a roughly-prepared mashed potato, with fish dishes, with poached eggs, and of course to dip chunky chips in!

2 large cloves garlic, crushed
2 large yolks from free-range hen's eggs
300ml (½ pint) olive oil (not extra virgin, as this adds bitterness)
Juice of ½ lemon
Seasoning

1) In a large bowl or food processor whisk the egg yolks and garlic vigorously until a smooth, emulsified and light consistency is achieved.

2) Now add the olive oil, drop by drop at first while still mixing continuously. Be patient at this stage, and just enjoy the process of making that deliciously thick relish. Keep adding the oil first drop by drop and then gradually, dribble by dribble. When you have used half of the oil the remainder can be added as a steady stream while you beat. The lemon juice can either be introduced during this process gradually to loosen the thick mixture or added at the end.

3) The mixture should now be thick in consistency and able to support itself. Taste and season with a little salt and pepper and serve.

THE ISLAND INGREDIENT

Pasties, Pies and Pizzas

Amaranthe crimping

PASTRYMAKING

As in breadmaking, there is a lot of myth surrounding the making of pastry: the terrors of hands-too-warm, cool slabs to roll one's pastry out on, and the worry about working the pastry too much. Generally, at the Bakery, plain flour is used to make both sweet and savoury pastries. However, we make perfectly good pastry with strong flour if we are out of plain. The proportions of most of our pastries are 2:1, the flour being double the quantity of fat used to bind the pastry together. We always make our pastries by hand as those made by machine have the fats incorporated too finely and produce tough pastries.

CORNISH PASTY PASTRY (WHITE FLOUR)

The amount of water used to bind in this recipe is approximately 50% of your flour weight, but be aware that different types of flour absorb different amounts of fluid, so don't assume you have the right amount and pour in the whole amount of liquid in one go!

enough for 8–9 large pasties · we use organic strong white but plain can be used.

1 kg (2 lb 4 oz) flour
500g (1 lb 2 oz) pastry margarine (Trex is a good fat for this pastry)
Water and seasoning

1)   Chop up the fat into small lumps, rub the fat into the flour using your fingertips, a washing up bowl is useful for mixing in. We are aiming at something towards a very rough breadcrumb consistency with a good scattering of small lumps of fat which will make your finished pastry light and flaky. In fact if all of the fat is too finely worked in you will have a tougher result.

2)   Add the water gradually and when the pastry is becoming to come together pull it towards you and squash down with the heel of your hand until all of the dry lumps are incorporated. Don't be afraid of working the pastry but stop when all of the dry bits are mixed in.

3)   Cling wrap the pastry and refrigerate for at least 20 min. to allow the elastic gluten present to relax and allow you later easy rolling. The pastry should be soft and silky in texture and have a general marbling of small lumps of fat visible which when cooked will produce a beautifully crisp flaky pastry. This dough will last for 3–4 days refrigerated.

QUICHE/HOMITY PASTRY (WHOLEMEAL/WHITE MIX)

For our quiches and homity pies we use a mixture of both organic white strong flour and organic stoneground wholemeal. These we use in 50:50 proportion to achieve a golden brown and nutty tasting pastry. Note the use of beaten egg and the precooking. As a result of this, you can forget those awful ceramic beans of yesteryear! They will only break your teeth if they remain undiscovered, and turn grandma into a kitchen roller-skater. Mine got thrown onto Moo Green, outside the bakery, years ago. No beanstalk yet, though!

for one quiche

400g (14 oz) flour, wholemeal and white in equal quantities.
200g (7 oz) pastry fat
Seasoning
Egg for glazing
Water

1) The method is much the same as for pasty pastry. Work in the fat, leaving some small lumps of fat to give a marbling texture.

2) Add the water conservatively; work with the heel of your hand until you have a consistently smooth pastry. Then cling-wrap and refrigerate to allow to relax. With the wholemeal flour in it, this pastry will only last for two or three days in the fridge before deteriorating.

3) Again because of the inclusion of wholemeal flour, the cooking of this pastry is aided by painting the raw pastry with beaten egg and precooking for five minutes in a hot oven.

4) There will be some trimming later to achieve that professional look to the finished quiche or pie. Roll out to fill a quiche dish and overlap the sides to be trimmed off when your quiche or pie has been cooked and cool enough to hold. Then, trim flush with the flan dish.

SWEETENED PASTRY

A very simple and quick sweet pastry employs a 4:2:1 ratio. To make enough pastry to fill a 30 cm (12-in) flan dish is therefore 400g (14 oz) of flour, 200g (7 oz) of a chosen fat and 100g (3½ oz) of caster sugar.
There is a sweet pastry recipe using eggs, *Pâte à Foncer*, on p. 122.

Another batch of pasties from Sean's production line!

A lot has been said and theorised about the Cornish pasty. Basically, it was a means of transforming sealed food to the workplace, be that the underground tin mines of Cornwall or the work fields of this verdant county. The ingredients would vary from house to house and village to village. The seasons would also dictate the filling, as turnips and swedes would only be available during the autumn and winter months, unless clamped, as would the beef which before refrigeration would traditionally be culled in the colder months of the year. We are lucky nowadays with refrigeration and a constant supply of vegetables year-round, so our pasties, second to none, are made with 50% local spuds, 25% white turnip, and 25% swede as far as the root vegetables are concerned. The filling of tender Tresco Island beef skirt or chuck steak makes our pasties moist and full of flavour. While the legal requirement in the UK is for only 13% meat, the 25% ratio of delicious chunks of that well-reared beef makes our pasties famous within the islands and keeps us in constant production to keep up with the huge demand!

This is the recipe for traditional Cornish pasties. Other favourites are crab with fresh dill; pork and apple; vegetarian with sweet peppers; and tarragon, beef and stilton. The crab dill ones we produce hardly even make the hot cabinet! Once again, any creations you wish to try are possible!

recipe makes 8 pasties · as a guide, each pasty requires 140–150g cooked vegetables and the same weight of meat

THE PASTRY

Use the recipe and the quantities on p. 110 to make a strong white flour pastry. Mix until soft but not sticky and cool in the fridge.

THE FILLING

600g (1 lb 4 oz) potatoes, good and waxy, diced small
1.2 kg (2 lb 8 oz) good quality diced beef skirt or chuck steak
300g (10 oz) swede, diced small
300g (10 oz) turnips, diced small
2 large onions, finely chopped
Vegetable oil
Salt and pepper

1) Fry the onions in oil. Set aside to cool. Boil the cubed vegetables until *al dente* in salted and peppered water, drain and set aside to cool. Mix with the browned onions.

2) Roll out the pastry on a floured surface, 5 mm (¼ in.) thick and cut into rounds approximately 20 cm, or 8 in.

3) Take a large cooking spoon and place a heaped amount of the cooled filling into the middle of the pastry round. Arrange a good handful of raw diced beef on top of the vegetables, which will allow the juices that the meat releases to moisten and flavour the vegetables during the cooking process. Season with salt and pepper.

4) Fold the side of pastry nearest to you away from you and press firmly down with your fingers to seal into a semicircle. If you are right-handed, start crimping with your index finger from the right-hand side; if left-handed, start at the left. Lift a little edge of pastry and press firmly down as you move your finger along the edge, creating an overlapping, travelling, crimp.

5) Glaze with beaten egg and bake on a well-greased tray at 200–220°C for 30 min., or until golden brown.

Soon after we opened at the Bakery, we became a place of discovery for the hungry continental sailors mooring around the shores of St Martins and appreciative of quality homecooked food. Most of our quiches, pies and flans contain onion as an integral ingredient and it was a desire to produce an onion-free tart that brought about the birth of our best-selling dish. It also gave those intrepid travellers some flavour of their homes long away. Aubergine has the most wonderful texture and flavour and while it is not an English regular it is most definitely a favourite in Mediterranean climes, along with tomato, sweet peppers and basil. The only onion in this dish is in our pizza sauce, which is added just to give flavour, not texture.

makes one 30 cm (12-in) tart, or eight slices

THE PASTRY

This is made following the recipe on p. 111, using 450g (1 lb) of strong white flour and adding a liberal sprinkling of oregano or marjoram, a small handful of sun-dried tomatoes for flavour and an attractive speckling effect, and two tablespoons of olive oil.

Add cold water to the mixture to bind into a soft but not sticky dough. Set aside in the fridge to chill and relax, while preparing the filling.

THE FILLING

For the main filling:
1 aubergine sliced into 1 cm rounds
3 tomatoes, sliced
A handful of diced mixed-colour sweet peppers
About 3 handfuls mozzarella and cheddar cheese in a 50:50 mix
Fresh basil
A handful of good pitted black olives
For the sauce:
1 shallot or small onion
1 clove garlic
Dried basil, oregano or marjoram
Olive oil
400g (14 oz) can organic chopped tomatoes

Splash of red wine vinegar
2 tbsp tomato purée

1) Fry the shallot or onion with the garlic and some dried basil, oregano or marjoram, in the olive oil. Set the oven to 220°C.

2) Add the chopped tomatoes, already blended to a sauce, plus a splash of red wine vinegar and the tomato purée. Heat gently.

3) Now roll out the pastry evenly and to a thickness of 5mm, into an oiled flan dish, folding over the edges to stop it shrinking whilst cooking. Paint with beaten egg and prebake for five minutes.

4) Fry the aubergines or bake them for about 15 min. on an olive-oiled tray, generously covered with more olive oil and a good sprinkling of dried basil.

5) Spread one ladle of the pasta sauce over the pastry base. Layer the baked aubergines on top of the sauce, and place the sliced tomatoes on top of these. Scatter the sweet peppers liberally over the tomatoes and add fresh basil at this stage if available. Dot evenly over the tomatoes with black olives and cover with grated cheese.

6) Bake for 20–25 min. at 200–220°C or until golden brown.

7) Trim the folded pastry edges away and eat either hot or cold, with a nice salad and vinaigrette dressing and a glass of good red wine!

I have researched and had many suggestions on the origins of this pie, which was suggested to me by an Island visitor many years ago. The West Country, Ireland, America and many others have been given as suggestions for its birthplace, but as far as I can glean this delicious pie was created by the groundbreaking Cranks organisation in London in the sixties. It is fantastic straight from the oven but also delicious cold with a salad. We have changed the original pastry recipe to one of half white and half organic wholemeal flour to make the base less heavy.

makes one 30 cm (12-in) pie

FOR THE PASTRY

400g (14 oz) wholemeal and white flours mixed 50:50
200g (7 oz) shortening or white fat (e.g. Trex)
150ml (¼ pint) water, approximately
1 tsp salt and a pinch of black pepper
1 whisked egg for glazing the base

PIE FILLING

1.25 kg (2 lb 12 oz) potatoes, peeled
1 onion, chopped
200g (7 oz) mature cheddar and some mozzarella
4 garlic cloves, crushed
A handful of roughly chopped parsley
A splash of milk and large knob of butter

1) Rub the shortening into the mix of flours, adding the salt, pepper, and then the water to make a smooth dough that is soft and not too dry to roll! Place the mix in a fridge to cool and relax.

2) Fry the onions and the garlic in some fat or vegetable oil until the onions are on the point of a golden-brown caramelised colour; this is imperative for the sweet onion flavour you need.

3) Meanwhile, chop the potatoes into rough chunks and boil them until tender in some salted water. Drain them and add the butter and a splash of milk, the roughly-chopped parsley and about half of the cheese. Mix into a rustic mash consistency with the onions and garlic.

3) Roll out the pastry to fit a well-greased 30 cm (12-in) flan dish with removable bottom, folding the pastry over the edges to prevent shrinking.

4) Bake this blind, with a painting of whisked egg to prevent shrinking and sogginess, for about 5 min. at 200–220°C.

5) Press the filling into the pastry base level with the top of the dish. Roughly spread the remainder of the cheese and add some more parsley for decoration. Some mozzarella over the top adds a lovely golden colour to the finished dish.

6) Keeping the oven at the same heat, bake for 25 min. or until golden brown. When cool, trim the folded pastry for that professional look. Cut and eat.

FLAKY PASTRY

Makes enough for one 30 cm (12-in) tart, as does the quick version on p. 122

225g (8 oz) pastry margarine such as Trex or a 50:50 mix of lard and butter, cubed into approximately 1 cm (1/2 inch) cubes.
400g (14oz) flour (we use strong white)
175ml–200ml (6–7 fl oz) cold water

1) Take a quarter of the fat and work into the flour till it resembles fine breadcrumbs. Add the water and mix to a soft pastry. Chill for 30 min.

2) Roll out the chilled pastry on a floured table to a rectangle about 30cm by 20 cm (12 x 8 inches). Divide the remaining fat into three equal portions.

3) Dot one portion of the fat on the middle and right hand side of the pastry. Fold the fatless left-hand side of the pastry over the middle and fold the other side on top of this, creating three layers. Leave to relax for some few minutes and roll out again.

4) Repeat the dotting, folding and rolling, with the other two portions of fat. Cling wrap and refrigerate for 30 min. before rolling.

At the Bakery we make a variety of thin-crust pizzas topped with a range of products. An enormous variety of toppings is of course possible: see below for our own ideas. Here is the basic pizza recipe we use.

for one 12-inch pizza. this will not look as though it will adequately feed two people, but it will! Red wine is a must to drink with pizza!

PIZZA BASE

400g (14 oz) strong white flour
1 tsp salt
2 tbsp olive oil
Herbs (marjoram, oregano, basil)
Water to bind (approx 200 ml, 7 fl oz)
A few sun-dried tomatoes, for flavour and speckling

PIZZA SAUCE

400g (14 oz) can chopped organic tomatoes, blended
4 tbsp tomato purée
1 tbsp red wine vinegar
½ onion and ½ sweet pepper
1 clove garlic
1 teaspoon salt
Herbs (marjoram/oregano)

1) Fry the onion, pepper and garlic in olive oil. When the onions are soft, add the other ingredients and bubble the sauce for at least half an hour for it to combine and thicken, using plenty of herbs as they will cook out—as will the garlic, of which more than one clove can be used if preferred.

PIZZA TOPPING

Basic pizza sauce as above
1 handful each chopped onion and sweet peppers
1 or 2 garlic cloves, crushed
Cheddar and mozzarella, in a 50:50 mix, to taste
Other items, to your choice (see opposite)

1)   Make the basic sauce as described.
2)   While this is cooking, mix the ingredients for the base into a smooth dough, not too wet, and refrigerate to relax.
3)   After cooking, allow the sauce to cool a little. Roll out the dough into a 30 cm (12") circle, about 5mm (¼-in) thick. If it is too elastic after your first attempt, allow the dough to relax for 10 min. Then place on either a well-greased pizza pan or baking tray.
4)   One ladle of sauce adequately covers the base. On top of this we place the ingredients listed as the basis of all our pizzas; the quantities are optional.
5)   A variety of ingredients can then be added to give the pizza its individual identity. These include mushrooms, capers (these go well with fish), salami, ham, chicken, our own smoked salmon, mullet and mackerel, anchovy, olives, tomatoes, vegetables in season and anything else that takes your fancy. The cheese we finish the pizza off with is a 50:50 mix of mozzarella and cheddar (and thus not too expensive).
5)   Finally, give the pizza a sprinkling of salt, a turn of black pepper and a liberal drizzle of olive oil. Cook at 200–220°C for 18 min., or until the cheese is nicely browned.
6)   Finally, remember not to put too many ingredients onto the pizza. Simplicity is best.

This is definitely my favourite savoury tart in the Bakery, begging to be eaten when cooled a little but still warm (Darcy, my daughter, also has a penchant for stealing a slice when my back is turned!). Its origins are in something called THE BOOK OF OLD TARTS, *by Elizabeth Hodder. After we developed the dish in the Bakery, we omitted the garlic from the tart description but not from the ingredients, and added tomato for a sharper flavour and more attractive finish. We now sell out every day we make it.*

Courgette flower

We use our mixed-flour pastry for this dish and the courgettes come from Ian Metcalf's abundant fields. Use a flan dish with a removable bottom.

makes one 30 cm (12-in) tart and cuts into eight good slices

Wholemeal and white mixed-flour pastry for one tart (see p. 111)
2 courgettes
60g (2 oz) butter
4 cloves garlic, crushed
Juice of ½ lemon
8 free-range eggs
A splash of double cream
200g (7 oz) blue cheese
3 regular-sized tomatoes, or equivalent amount of cherry tomatoes, for decoration
Pinch of tarragon
Seasoning

1) Roll out the pastry on a floured table to fit a greased flan dish.
2) Glaze with beaten egg and prebake for five minutes, while you assemble the rest of the ingredients.
3) Slice the courgettes widthways, into about 5mm (¼-in) rounds.
4) Melt the butter in a large pan and sauté the courgettes, add seasoning, crush

in the garlic and cook for five more minutes. While the pan is still on the heat add a teaspoon of English mustard and the seasoning, and squeeze in the lemon juice.

5) Stir and sizzle for a minute and enjoy the aromatic flavours released.

6) Set the mixture aside while you beat the eggs, grated blue cheese and cream together. Add black pepper.

7) Arrange the courgette, garlic, lemon filling on the precooked base. Pour the beaten egg and cream mixture on top.

8) Decorate with tomato slices and a sprinkling of fresh or dried tarragon and bake at 200–220°C for 20–25 min. or until golden brown.

MAKING FRESH PASTA

makes enough for 4 · make 8 hours before using
requires pasta machine to roll out

250g (9 oz) pasta flour (or strong white flour)
5 tbsp olive oil
2 tbsp water
5 egg yolks
1 whole egg
A pinch of salt

1) To a small mixing bowl add the egg yolks, whole egg, water, oil and salt. Whisk together until the yolks have broken.

2) Place the flour in a food blender or mixer, and turn on. Slowly add the egg mix until the dough starts to come together. Stop the machine and check it from time to time, for the dough has to stay together and not get too wet. To get to the next stage you might not need to use all the egg mix.

3) Once the dough is soft and silky, workable to the finger, leave it to rest in the fridge for at least 8 hours.

4) Now roll the pasta through a pasta machine, working down to number 2 (or the second last to finest). Leave to rest on bench for 3 min.

5) Then using the preferred attachment—tagliatelle if you are doing the recipe on p. 140 or noodle if the one on p. 130—and roll the pasta sheet through.

6) Blanch off the pasta in boiling salted water for 20 sec. Remove from pan into iced water till chilled, then take pasta out of water. Put it into a tub with a little olive oil and mix carefully (this will stop the pasta from sticking).

SWEET PASTRY: *PÂTE À FONCER*

PÂTE À FONCER

This is the recipe we use to make Lemon Tarts (p. 164), Tarte Tatin (p. 166) and the wonderful Apple and Island Blackberry Pie (p. 172) that we create when the Island is awash with bulging blackberries and thrushes sit atop bramble bushes with purple beaks.
It is a rich, short and delicate pastry, so we use plain flour for this recipe. We do not prebake this pastry; the butter in the mix aids its cooking.

makes one 30 cm (12-in) or 24 small tarts

500g (1 lb 2 oz) plain flour
250g (9 oz) chilled butter (we use salted)
50g (2 oz) caster sugar
1 egg yolk
80 ml (3½ fl oz) water

1)   Cube the butter into small lumps. Put the flour into a large bowl, mix in the sugar thoroughly and then make a well in the top.

2)   Place the butter and the egg yolk into the well in the flour and with your fingertips work the butter into the flour, gradually drawing in the flour until you have a fine breadcrumb-like mixture throughout. Gradually add the water and knead with your hands to achieve a soft silky consistency.

3)   Don't be afraid to add more water to achieve this softness, for if the pastry is too dry it will crack later when you try to roll it out. Cling-wrap and refrigerate to allow it to relax.

QUICK FLAKY PASTRY

a speedy alternative to the recipe on p. 117. Makes one 30cm (12-in) tart

To make a quick flaky pastry, chill a 225g (8 oz) block of pastry margarine such as Trex or a 50:50 mix of butter and lard in the freezer for about 30 min. Grate the chilled fat into 400g (14oz) flour (we use strong white bread flour) season and add 175–200ml (6-7 fl oz) of cold water and mix gently, and coolly, to a soft pastry. Chill, wrapped, in the fridge for 30 min. before rolling.

ROVING CHEF

"*F*irst of all I travelled with my good friend Brad. We went to Singapore and Thailand for a month. This was my first experience of Thailand, an amazing country. The food and produce is completely different from what I was used to, but the depth of flavour is there despite the different cooking processes. The fruits are especially juicy, bright in colour and flavour. The open-air markets and the smells were amazing, and I longed to work a little while I was there—something that would happen at the end of these travels.

"After the month was up, and we'd moved on to Oz, I took a job at Mariners, a seafood restaurant and bar on Hamilton Island. Working with seafood is probably my biggest passion now, and going back to living on an island for three months was also appealing to me. The seafood down under is similar to the produce of home but although the shellfish didn't have as much flavour as here, the fish was just as good—only on some occasions seven or eight times the size.

"A customer had been out fishing, and came into the restaurant asking if he could bring in a mackerel he had caught, for us to prepare and serve for eight of his guests. Stephan, the head chef, was off that morning and I was in charge, so I accepted the man's offer and he went off to get his fish. I thought surely one mackerel wasn't going to feed eight people; he must have caught a few. He returned half an hour later with one king Spanish mackerel, one and a half meters in length!

"My next move would take me to Melbourne. The Oslo hotel and hostel in St Kilda was a nice, cheap place, which over the next five months would bring a lot to me in the way of friends, good times and support. I was sat watching a movie with a couple of Canadian guys, when three Swedish girls walked into the hostel social room asking for one more helper to pick grapes at a vineyard. Of course my hand went straight up, and the next day we hired a car for the week and off we went. The small vineyard was in Ballarat, a couple of hours' drive from the hostel. Run by a family who grew all the vines organically, we got straight into picking the grapes. After lunch we would go back into the fields. The girls would go back to picking the grapes but John (the owner) and I would put the grapes through the de-stalker and check the wines at the different stages. This was really interesting to me. I grew a new fondness for wine and appreciated it a lot more.

"Next, I was to take the junior sous-chef position at the Bluestone Restaurant on Flinders Lane: a nice restaurant with a great bar downstairs, and happy family-like vibes among the staff. I would work on the meat, fish and sauce section; working with the Sous. Before long I realised we knew the same places and even had some of the same friends. Working Monday to Friday was nice as well, so I ended up having a good social life inside and outside of work. I had my twenty-first birthday in Melbourne.

"Leaving Melbourne, I was now to travel for three months through New Zealand, Singapore, Malaysia, Thailand and Cambodia. In New Zealand, I would meet some relatives of mine. My uncle Mike used to be a chef, and we'd talk of international cuisine and whose was best. I started missing working, and on travelling from Wellington up to Rotarua I went via Napier, on the coast. I found a nice little place, ordered lunch and talked to the chef afterwards, and he showed me how he did the dessert (pineapple pudding). I then realised this was a great way to learn, and travelling through Singapore, Malaysia, Thailand and Cambodia I would do this a few times.

"In Cambodia, I would work with Vietnamese mint, a spicy herb which works fantastically in curried dishes. In Thailand I would learn of Thai basil, again completely different from our basil. Thai basil is fresher in flavour with an aniseed twist. I would cook with fresh lychees for the first time, and also Thai oysters—which have so much more body and flavour than our slimy friends over here.

Then in Malaysia, I would learn how they cook the spices out for a good twenty minutes before adding the flesh of the fish or meat—a way I had never cooked before, for in western cooking we always seal the meat, then add the spices. In broken English, the Malaysian chef who tried my version of his dish, cooked the western way, would tell me that my spices were raw and the texture of my sauce was grainy.

"This to me is the international cuisine which everyone talks about. It's not just about putting beef stew on the same plate as some spicy noodles. It's actually getting out there and experiencing the cooking methods that everyone uses. In cooking there is no real right or wrong—just good or bad.

"Right now, I'm in India with my girlfriend Thea, to whom I dedicate my contribution to THE ISLAND INGREDIENT."

PAULIE WEBSDALE

Main Courses from the Seven Stones

Pollack

THE ISLAND INGREDIENT

BEER-BATTERED FISH AND CHIPS

Everybody loves fish and chips, and here is my spin on a classic British take-away dish. Ian Mitchell lands large pollack for me which he catches just off the group of rocks between Scilly and the mainland called the Seven Stones. Chip size and thickness is a personal choice. Some people like the skin on (I do); some don't.

the batter is enough to coat 4–5 fillets but otherwise the quantities are your choice

BEER BATTER

> 200g (7 oz) plain flour
> 450 ml (1 pint) of bitter
> 1 tbsp mirin*
>   or white wine vinegar
> 1 tbsp soy sauce
> 1 tsp salt
> ½ tsp white pepper

1) Sift the flour and in a large mixing bowl add the salt and pepper, soy sauce and mirin or vinegar.

2) Add two-thirds of the beer to the bowl and stir in, adding more if required, until a thick sticky consistency is achieved.

TARTARE SAUCE

Use the recipe on page 106, in the quantities given.

HOME-CUT CHIPS

1) Cut chips to desired size, allowing 2 or 3 large potatoes per portion. Place in a large saucepan with cold salted water, bring up to the boil, turn down

*Mirin is an essential condiment used in Japanese cuisine, with 40%–50% sugar. It is a kind of rice wine similar to sake, but with a lower alcohol content—14% instead of 20%.

128

THE ISLAND INGREDIENT

to simmer. Once a knife passes through them easily, drain into a colander. How soon this happens will depend on the size of the chip.

2) Whether you have a fryer or a chip pan, the oil wants to be 180°C. Fry the chips until the desired colour is achieved.

3) Lift the chips for 2–3 min., then place back in oil for 1 min. This will help to crisp up your chips. Shake well and season with salt.

TO FRY THE FISH

1) Season the piece of fish you are using (we use pollack, an inexpensive white-flesh fish with a beautiful flavour and flaky texture) then dust it with flour. One fillet per person should be adequate.

2) Dip it in the batter mixture. Once coated, place half the fish under the hot oil until it starts to float, then let go. This will help to prevent it sticking.

3) Once the desired colour of the batter is achieved and the fish is floating (which means it is cooked), take it out, shake well and place on top of chips with a big dollop of tartare sauce. If you have them, add a lemon wedge and some fresh leaves.

Goldeneye mullet is a type of grey mullet, a fish which is mostly overlooked on the mainland. It has a glorious colour, firm texture and fantastic flavour. In the height of the season fishermen can net hundreds at a time so when they come knocking at my kitchen door with the fish still flapping I jump at the chance to put this one on the menu!

serves 4

DRESSINGS

Prepare the reduced balsamic dressing and one of the herb oils (see p. 101)

EGG-FRIED NOODLES

200g (7 oz) fresh pasta (p. 121)
  rolled through the noodle cutter and then blanched
3 red peppers, deseeded and cut into strips
3 large carrots, peeled and cut into fine strips
2 medium-sized red onions, sliced
2 cloves crushed garlic
50g (1¾ oz) sesame seeds
2 large free-range eggs
30g (1 oz) roughly-chopped coriander
15ml (1 tbsp) soy sauce

1) To a hot wok, add a little oil until it is smoking. Throw in onions and garlic and cook until lightly caramelised.
2) Add the peppers and carrots. Fry for 1 min., then add soy sauce until the mixture reduces.
3) Add cooked pasta to wok. Stir around until pasta is hot, then crack in the eggs quickly, stirring and mixing the noodles.
4) Finish noodles with sesame seeds and coriander, and check for seasoning.

LIGHT CURRY SAUCE

50g (1¾ oz) chopped shallots
1 clove garlic, crushed

1 tbsp fresh ginger, grated
1 tsp cumin powder
1 tsp medium Madras curry powder
½ tsp turmeric
200 ml (7 fl oz) coconut milk

1) In a little oil, sweat shallot and garlic until soft—no colour—then add ginger and cook out.
2) Now add cumin, curry powder and turmeric. Cook for 1 min. At this point it's important not to let the spices burn, so keep stirring.
3) Now add the coconut milk. Turn down to a simmer, and cook out for 5 min. Leave sauce to cool.

TO COOK THE MULLET

As you can see in the picture, I have cut the fish down the centre of the fillet, for a different shape and to achieve more height when laid on the noodles. The mullet is seasoned and pan fried in pomace/vegetable oil, skin side down at first, for two-three minutes on each side until crisp and golden brown. I have also used some mizuna salad leaves as a garnish.

We use Arborio rice at the Seven Stones, and we accompany many different dishes with a risotto. Some examples are Chicken with Saffron and Pinenut Risotto, John Dory with Asparagus and Broad Bean Risotto, and the John Dory and Caramelised Onion Risotto on page 134.

SCILLONIAN LOBSTER, CRAWFISH AND CRAB RISOTTO

Shellfish is hard to come by on the mainland, and is often rather expensive, so when I have this dish on in the pub, it's not there for long. Shellfish is a massive part of the local economy down here on the Isles of Scilly, and a tasty one too.

PHOTO: AMARANTHE FROST

200g (7 oz) Arborio rice
400ml (14 fl oz) shellfish stock or water
200g (7 oz) diced shallot
2 cloves garlic, crushed
25g (1 oz) butter
60ml (3 fl oz) white wine
30ml (1¾ fl oz) double cream
20g (1 oz) grated parmesan
Juice of ½ a lemon
15g (2 tbsp) freshly chopped chives
1 medium lobster tail,
   cooked and diced
500g (1 lb 2 oz) cooked diced crawfish tail
300g (10 oz) fresh white crab meat

1) In a heavy-bottomed saucepan, heat up a little oil and sweat the shallot and garlic for 5 min., ceasing before there is any colour to it.

2) Add the rice and sweat for a further 2 min. Then add the wine and reduce to nothing.

3) Add the stock or water, hot, a ladleful at a time. The risotto will be ready in 18–20 min.

4) Once the rice is cooked, remove pan from heat. Add the diced shellfish, plus a good squeeze of lemon juice, and stir in. Then add the butter, cream and parmesan to finish. Check seasoning.

5) Finally, stir some freshly chopped chives through the dish, and serve.

CURRIED SWEET POTATO AND MIZUNA RISOTTO

200g (8 oz) Arborio rice
400ml (1 pint) vegetable
    stock
200g (8 oz) diced shallot
2 cloves garlic, crushed
25g (1 oz) butter
60ml (4 tbsp) white wine
2 large sweet potatoes
1 tbsp garam masala
1 tsp ground cumin
¼ tsp cayenne pepper
¼ tsp turmeric

Mizuna

1)   Peel both sweet potatoes and chop one into large chunks. Drizzle with melted butter and roast in the oven at 180°C for twenty minutes.

2)   Dice the other sweet potato into 5mm (¼ in.) pieces and pan fry in butter with the spices.

3)   Now make a basic risotto, using instructions 1–3 opposite, substituting vegetable stock if you wish to keep this a vegetarian dish. Pass the roasted sweet potato through a fine sieve and combine it with the rice dish as the stock is being added.

4)   Mix in the softened pan-fried curried potato at the end of the cooking process and fold in gently. Serve with salad-dressed mizuna and decorate with chopped coriander.

5)   There's no cheese in this recipe; the wine should make it sweet and tasty.

FETA CHEESE AND SPINACH RISOTTO

Spinach is abundant on St Martin's throughout the whole season, both the type grown in our fields and sea spinach—collected as it grows, wild, at the tops of our golden beaches (and illustrated on p. 25).

Following instructions 1–3 opposite, we combine about 200g (8 oz) of washed, destalked and chopped spinach around half way through the cooking of the risotto and add the same weight of feta cheese cut into small cubes and folded in as the dish leaves the pan. A grating or two of parmesan cheese to decorate, some torn basil leaves and a sprinkling of chopped sun-dried tomatoes make it colourful as well as delicious!

JOHN DORY WITH CARAMELISED RED ONION AND SAFFRON RISOTTO, LEMON PURÉE AND SUN-BLUSHED TOMATOES

John Dory is one of my favourite fish, and if you are cooking for your friends at a dinner party it will excite your guests. If you take your fish filleted from your fishmonger, you are left with a tasty, boneless piece of fish. Using one fillet a portion, and preparing the lemon purée and sun-blushed tomatoes beforehand, this dish can be finished in twenty minutes on the night, full of colour and flavour, this is a great dish to impress! There is a larger picture of this dish on page 125.

CARAMELISED RED ONION AND SAFFRON RISOTTO

Serves 4

200g (7 oz) Arborio rice
400 ml (14 fl oz) chicken stock
1 large red onion
2 medium cloves garlic
25g (1 oz) butter
60ml (2 fl oz) white wine
30ml (1 fl oz) double cream
20g (3/4 oz) grated parmesan
1 large pinch saffron strands

1) Slice the red onion and purée the garlic cloves. Put a heavy-based saucepan on the stove, and in a little oil sweat the onion until golden colour is obtained. Add the garlic and sweat for 1 further minute.

2) Add rice to pan, keep stirring for 2 min., and then add wine until all is absorbed.

3) Infuse saffron into hot chicken stock, and add it a ladleful at a time, stirring occasionally. Turn heat down to a simmer.

4) After 18–20 min., the rice will have absorbed the liquid and is ready to be finished.

5) Take pan off the heat add a little cream and the parmesan. Season to taste. The risotto is ready to serve immediately.

SIMPLE SUN-BLUSHED TOMATOES

Use the recipe given on p. 107, in the quantities given there. This part can be done days before the dish is to be served. The tomatoes can be stored in the fridge, left in the oil, for up to one week.

LEMON PURÉE

This purée will keep for 2 to 3 days, so can be done well before and kept in the fridge until the dish is going to be served.

8 fresh lemons, peeled, retaining the peel
110 ml (4 fl oz) water
20g (¾ oz) sugar
100 ml (½ fl oz) extra virgin olive oil
Lemon juice to taste
Additional water for initial blanching

1) Place lemon skin in 2 litres (3½ pints) of cold water and bring to the boil for 5 min. Drain through a sieve and repeat this process four times.
2) Drain and liquidise with the sugar, adding the water and olive oil slowly.
3) Squeeze in fresh lemon juice to taste and pass through a fine sieve.
4) Season with salt and a little cayenne pepper.
5) Serve chilled.

TO PREPARE THE FINISHED PLATE

1) Place risotto in the middle of the plate with teardrops of lemon purée round it. Place five sun-blushed tomatoes around the plate with caper berries in between.

Okahijiki

2) Put John Dory fillet on top of risotto. Sprinkle chives around the plate, put two baby carrots on top of the fish, with desired lettuce leaf (I've used red mustard leaf, which in our case comes from Ian Metcalf) and put some sprigs of okahijiki around the outside.

This is a great starter, or may be just something to have on a platter at a buffet. I first started gravadlaxing my own salmon while working not far from the River Tay at a country house hotel near Blairgowrie, but my second chef Kris, who worked with me there, is a true master! Most places offer smoked salmon, which is usually bought in and the flavour can be dull. Although the fish is rarely caught here—we use organic Scottish—we give this type of curing a unique Seven Stones twist.

This is a favourite of my dad's at Christmas, and as you can see in the picture opposite we keep it simple. Serve with some granary bread—and use Thai basil (see p. 124) if you can get it.

for 1 side of salmon

DILL MUSTARD DRESSING

This dressing is simple, but goes very well with the salmon. Use the recipe on p. 104.

GRAVADLAX

1 side of salmon
225g (8 oz) brown sugar
150g (5 oz) table salt
40g (1 ½ oz) honey
75ml (3 fl oz) whisky
25g (just under 1 oz) fresh dill
5g (1 tbsp) fresh basil,
   preferably Thai basil

1) First, cut the fillet of salmon in half (top to bottom).
2) In a mixing bowl, mix together the salt, sugar and chopped herbs, and in a measuring jug mix the honey and whisky.
3) Then line a tray with tinfoil, lay one half of the salmon on the foil, skin side down.
4) Pour a quarter of the whisky solution on the fish and massage it in, then pour half the salt/sugar mix on top and rub it in again.
5) Then pour half the whisky solution on and put the rest of the salt/sugar mix

on top.

6) Put the other half of the salmon fillet on top of this, flesh-side down. Then, with the skin facing you, pour the last quarter of whisky on top.

7) Wrap with tinfoil, then cling-film. Press between two trays in the fridge for three days.

8) Remove from the fridge, wash off the salt and sugar and any other liquid, and then dry well with a clean table cloth.

9) The salmon is then good to go. I personally think it is at its best three days after it has been washed off and rested again in the fridge.

Kris with his beloved salmon

DARCY'S DELICIOUS AUBERGINE LASAGNE

A green top for this recipe as it is from the Bakery, not the Seven Stones. Each October we head for the warm climes, delicious wines and fantastic food in Tuscany. Our gastronomic holidays are spent sightseeing, shopping for food and planning and preparing that fantastic evening meal to be enjoyed in our hilltop farmhouse, as the sun drops behind the roaming deer and silhouetted castles in that beautifully undulating landscape.

With the aid of Stephanie Alexander and Maggie Beer's TUSCAN COOKBOOK, Darcy (below) created this beautiful dish with an unusual twist. Rather than grilling the aubergine, she smoked the slices over our log fire to give this dish a fantastic flavour. Back on St Martin's, I'd do them in my smoker, but improvising in Italy she simply smoked them in a folding wire griddle tray. You can do them on a barbecue if you prefer. Next she scattered the surface of the prepared lasagne with cherry tomatoes, parmesan and buffalo mozzarella (as in the photo opposite), creating a beautifully sharp and lush-tasting lasagne.

serves 6

4 large aubergines cut into 5 mm (¼-in) slices
750g (14oz) lasagne sheets (2 packs)

CREAM SAUCE

6 cloves garlic
600ml (2 tubs) double cream
Ground black pepper
Ground sea salt
1 large handful roughly-chopped flat-leaf parsley

BÉCHAMEL SAUCE

See p. 104. Add a spoonful or two of grated parmesan to give it bite.

THE TOPPING

10 cherry tomatoes, halved
100g (3½ oz) grated parmesan
1 small pack buffalo mozzarella, sliced

1) Smoke the aubergine slices over a log fire until soft but not dried out, if at all possible; otherwise grill or fry them slowly, watching they neither get too oily nor dry out.

2) Cook the lasagne sheets in boiling water with a tablespoon of olive oil added, keeping the pan stirred to prevent the sheets from sticking together. Do not overcook, and when ready drain and refresh the sheets in cold water for later use.

3) To make the cream sauce, simply crush or finely chop the garlic into the cream, bubble gently on the stove for 5 min. Now add the chopped parsley, season and set aside.

4) Line an ovenproof dish with the refreshed lasagne sheets. Over these pour a quarter of the béchamel sauce. On top of the sauce, place a layer of the aubergine slices. Pour over this a quarter of the cream sauce.

5) Repeat this layering of the ingredients until you have created four layers. Scatter the surface with chopped cherry tomatoes, parmesan and mozzarella.

6) Bake at 200°C for 30 min.

7) Allow it to rest for 15 min. before cutting, as it will be very hot; meanwhile, open a bottle of *Pinot Grigio*!

WILD MUSHROOM TAGLIATELLE WITH GRILLED GOAT'S CHEESE

I really enjoy making fresh pasta; it's so much more rewarding once you've produced an entire dish from scratch. My recipe is given on page 121. Pasta is an obvious vegetarian option, but there are plenty more vegetarian dishes on the Seven Stones menu, including fresh taboulehs, different risottos (see pp. 132–4), puy lentil dhal (see p. 144) and so on.

serves 4 · if using homemade pasta, it needs to be left 8 hours before use.

TAGLIATELLE

Use the recipe on page 121 if you fancy fresh pasta, in which case you should allow 100g pasta per person. If using dried pasta, allow 125g per person.

PASTA SAUCE

200g (7 oz) mixed wild mushrooms
6 sunblushed tomatoes (see the John Dory recipe)
2 medium red onions, sliced
2 cloves garlic, crushed
3 large carrots, peeled and cut into fine strips
100ml (4 fl oz) white wine
250ml (9 fl oz) double cream
50g (2 oz) grated parmesan
30g (1 oz) butter
Chopped chives to garnish

1) In a large, hot frying pan, sweat the onions and garlic in a little oil until soft. Next add the sliced wild mushrooms and carrot with the butter and cook out for a further 5 min.

2) Now add the sunblushed tomatoes, followed by the white wine, and by further cooking reduce by two-thirds.

3) Add double cream, bring to boil, then turn down to a simmer.
4) At this point add the cooked tagliatelle. Mix through, then add grated parmesan and chopped chives.
5) Taste and check the seasoning. If the sauce is a little sticky add a little more cream.

TO FINISH

As you can see, in the picture, I have placed the tagliatelle in the centre of the bowl and I have used a grilled Gevrik goats cheese on top. Gevrik is from the West Country and is a tasty, smooth creamy goats cheese, I have also used some tarragon herb oil (see p. 100) and have used a few shavings of fresh parmesan.

For a guide to US measures, see pp 169, 171 and 187.

ROAST CHICKEN ON ISLAND POTATO SALAD WITH WHITE WINE SAUCE

Chicken is a staple on most menus. It's always a seller for us and in summer this is a nice dish, not too heavy, full of local produce (all the vegetables), and has nice bright colours.

serves 4

POTATO SALAD

5 large potatoes, peeled and diced
1 large red onion, sliced
1 clove of garlic, crushed
4 spring onions
2 sticks of celery, peeled, washed and diced small
Mayonnaise

1) Put potatoes in a saucepan with cold salted water. Bring to boil, turn down and cook for 5–10 min. or until potatoes are cooked. Then add sliced red onion and garlic. Leave for 30 sec., then drain, move to a bowl, and set aside.
2) When cool, add the diced celery and chopped spring onions. Bind with mayonnaise and season with salt and black pepper.

WHITE WINE SAUCE

1 onion
1 clove garlic
1 carrot
2 sticks of celery
1 chicken carcass
100ml (3½ fl oz) white wine
150ml (¼ pint) double cream
1 sprig of tarragon

1) With the chicken carcass cut into small pieces and in a saucepan, add half the onion and the carrot and celery. Bring to the boil in 2 litres (3½ pints) of water, turn down to a simmer and leave for 2 hours. Then strain (retain

the liquid but discard the carcass).

2) In a separate saucepan fry off the other half of the onion and garlic in a little butter until soft, with no colour.

3) Add wine and reduce by two thirds.

4) Add chicken stock and reduce on the stove, down to approximately 250ml (½ pint).

5) Now add the double cream. Bring just to the boil, turn down and reduce to sauce consistency. In a liquidiser or blender add the tarragon. Blend, pass and season.

TO FINISH

1) Set oven to 180°C. Using one breast per portion, give the chicken breast good colour on its skin side in a frying pan. Turn it over and place in the oven for 8–10 min., depending on the size of breast.

2) As you can see in the picture I have used baby carrots, mangetout and fine beans that I get from Ian Metcalf. I also used okahijiki, which I get from Ian, to garnish the plate, and have drizzled the sauce around.

Monkfish is a meaty fish, with a lovely texture. I like to leave the monkfish on the bone as this gives more flavour and holds a nice shape. Monkfish tails often come to my back door at the Seven Stones and when they do, they're always from a large fish with tails normally coming in at between four and five kilos.

The dhal recipe is a good vegetarian option on its own. I got this recipe in Malaysia, and I have added some spices and removed the ones which where hard for me to find. It's a tasty alternative to potatoes or rice and is just as easy. It will certainly impress your dinner guests. In the picture, I have used both the light curry sauce and balsamic dressing (see p. 101), and have garnished it with sunblushed tomato and mizuna.

serves 4   ·   allow 200g (7 oz) fish per person

PUY LENTIL DHAL

150g (5 oz) carrots
300g (10½ oz) Puy lentils
1 large red onion, sliced
3 cloves garlic, crushed
1 tsp Madras curry powder
1 tsp ground cumin
½ tsp turmeric
2 crushed whole cardamoms
400ml (14 fl oz) coconut milk
Oil for frying

1) Peel and cut the carrots into small pieces. Overcook in a pan of water so that they are soft enough to mash. Drain and set aside.

2) Put the puy lentils in a saucepan, add 500ml (just under 1 pint) of water and bring to the boil. Strain and refresh the lentils with cold water to remove any scum.

3) Now put lentils back in the saucepan. Cover with 750ml (1¼ pints) of water, bring to the boil, and then turn down to a simmer.

4) After 10 or 12 min.—whenever the lentils are just about ready—remove half of them and cool quickly. Cook the over half for a further 10 to 20 min.

until completely soft. Drain the water off.

5) In a separate saucepan, fry off the sliced red onion and crushed garlic in a little oil for 5 min. until soft and with a little colour. Now add the curry powder, cumin, turmeric and cardamom. Cook out for a further 3 min.

6) Add the carrots and continue cooking till they break down, then add the overcooked lentils and coconut milk. Bring to boil and turn down to a simmer.

7) Stirring occasionally, keep this pan on a low heat for a further 10–15 mins.

8) Remove from the heat and blend in a food processor.

9) Lastly, empty the mix into a bowl, mix in the lightly-cooked lentils, and check the seasoning.

COOKING THE MONKFISH

The cooking times depend on the size of the piece of fish, but if you're roasting it on the bone you should be looking at a 200g (7 oz) portion. To do this in a hot pan in a little oil, you should colour the flesh on all sides, then place in oven at 180°C for 6–7 min. To check the monkfish is cooked either use a temperature probe or touch. The fish should be slightly springy with a temperature of at least 43°C.

CALAMARI SALAD

This is a popular dish at the Seven Stones.
The squid I get in comes from St Mary's the same day it's landed, from Martin Bond.
While I was working in Melbourne, Australia, I picked up on this style of cooking the squid. The trick is to cook it quickly, as if you cook it for too long it will become chewy.

serves 4–6 · requires advance preparation and last-minute cooking

THE CALAMARI

4 medium-sized squid
30 ml (2 tbsp) sweet chilli sauce
30 ml (2 tbsp) mirin (see p. 128)
15 ml (1 tbsp) soy sauce
30 ml (2 tbsp) sunflower oil
Plain flour for dusting
Oil for deep frying

1) If you are cooking at home, I would ask your fishmonger to prepare the squid, but make sure you take the tentacles as well. So cut the tentacles into 1 in. pieces, and the squid tubes into rings.
2) Mix the chilli, mirin, soy sauce and sunflower oil in a container, put the prepared squid into the marinade and leave for at least 12 hours.
3) When you're ready to serve, have oil for deep frying set at about 180°C, take the squid out of the marinade, give a good dust in the flour, and quickly cook until colour is achieved. This should take about 30 sec. Place squid on a piece of kitchen cloth to absorb any extra oil, season with salt.

TO SERVE

The choice of the salad is completely up to you, but the salad dressing I use for this dish is the simple oil and lemon one given on page 102.
Place the squid around and on top of the salad. I also like to serve it with some fresh lime wedges, as in the photograph on the next page.

TATIN DEUX SAUMONS (TWO-SALMON TATIN)

A contribution using flaky pastry from Marie in Grenoble (see p. 164) .

makes one 30 cm (12-in) tatin
for pastry use either the recipe on p. 117 or the quick one on p. 122

Flaky pastry in the quantity given in the recipe
5 slices of smoked salmon
400g (14 oz) fresh salmon, diced
400g (14 oz) fromage blanc
4 eggs
Fresh dill
1-2 tbsp crushed 'baies roses' (pink peppercorns)

1) Line a 30 cm (12-in) pie dish with the smoked salmon. Mix all the other loose ingredients together. Pour over lined smoked salmon, then roll and place the flaky pastry over the top.

2) Cook at 180–200°C for about 25 min. or until the pastry is golden. Take out of oven, free the edges and flip over. Remove dish carefully.

Turbot is another of my favourite fish. I first worked with a whole turbot while working in the fish section at Whatley Manor, a time in my career when I grew fond of working with whole fish.

In this dish, instead of removing the fillets, which is normal restaurant practice, I've cut my turbot into steaks—giving more visual appearance and making it easier on the pocket!

CITRUS DRESSING AND HOLLANDAISE SAUCE

Use the recipes on pp. 103 and 105 respectively.

CONFIT PEPPERS

The method below gives a way of preserving peppers and adds a different texture to the dish; for speed, you could just fry the peppers.

1 red, 1 yellow and 1 green pepper
200 ml (7 fl oz) pomace oil/vegetable oil

1)   Peel and deseed peppers. You can now either cut them into even strips, season them and place in the oil in a small saucepan, or keep them whole. If you choose the strips, heat them until the oil starts to bubble, then remove from heat and leave to cool. Whole peppers will need submerging in deep fat at 80°C until they're soft. Either way, you can now keep these in the oil, in a jar, preserved.

2)   Remove peppers from oil to serve.

SWEET POTATO CRISPS

1 large sweet potato
Oil for shallow frying

1) Peel the sweet potato and discard the peel. Peel some strips off the potato, now taking off the flesh and saving these for frying as crisps.

2) If you have a fryer you need it at 140°C. Place the potato 'crisps' in the fryer (if you don't have a fryer you'll have to guess temperature and do a little at a time in a shallow frying pan) until all bubbles are gone and a golden colour is achieved.

4) Remove from pan onto a piece of kitchen towel to drain off any excess oil, then season with salt.

COOKING THE TURBOT

1) Use 200–250g (7–8 oz) of fish. Pan fry in a little oil, skin side down, until crisp; turn over and fry the other side until coloured. Place in oven at 180°C for 6–7 min. until springy but firm (or 43°C, as with the monkfish on p. 145).

TO FINISH

In the picture I have fried some okahijiki in a little butter and placed the fish on top. I have also used some orange segments. Often I will serve some buttered new potatoes on the side of this dish.

When we order our rump steaks from Tresco they come in whole, which is great for me as I can cut decent steaks and with the trim make this dish. to me it would be a winter dish, yet it seems to sell whenever it's on the menu. This is my spin on a classic French recipe; the sweet potato gnocchi is also different from the normal potato gnocchi. A great dish if you are cooking for a larger dinner party; I've served with spinach and peppers in the photo.

serves 6

3 slices smoked streaky bacon, cut into strips
600g (1lb 5 oz) diced beef
150ml (¼ pint) red wine
I cube beef bouillon or one beef oxo cube
2 cloves garlic, crushed
200g (7 oz) sliced onion
400g (14 oz) small cup button mushrooms, halved
Plain flour for dusting

1) Dust the diced beef in plain flour and in a hot large saucepan fry it off in a little oil until a nice colour is achieved on the beef. Now add the strips of bacon, onion and garlic, and cook out.

2) Add the red wine and stir in. Reduce. Mix the bouillon cube in 250 ml (9 fl oz) boiling water and add to saucepan.

3) Now turn down to a simmer and cook until beef is tender (about 1½ hours). Then add button mushrooms and cook on a low heat for a further 15 min. If the stew is a little thin, reduce down to the consistency you like— or you could cheat by using a bit of bisto at the end!

SWEET POTATO GNOCCHI

750g (1 lb 10 oz) sweet potato
300g (10½ oz) plain flour
25g (1 oz) butter
I egg yolk

1) Cut the sweet potatoes lengthways and place on a roasting tray skin side down. Season and roast in an oven at 200°C, until a knife passes through them easily (1–1½ hours). The outside may be black, but the inside delicious.

2) While potatoes are still warm, peel flesh away from the skin and put into a mixing bowl. Mash until smooth. Now beat in the flour, butter and egg yolk, and season with salt and pepper. Mix into a smooth dough.

3) Turn out the dough onto a floured surface and knead lightly once or twice. If the dough is still sticky, add more flour. Cut the dough into pieces 2cm x 3cm.

4) Bring a pan of salted water to the boil. Add dough balls, bring water back to the boil, and then turn down to a simmer. When the gnocchi float (around 3 min.), remove from pan with a slotted spoon and place on a tea towel to drain off any excess water.

TO FINISH

1) I like to roast my gnocchi in a little butter. To do this, heat a frying pan, add a little butter and add cooked and drained gnocchi, frying until they are crispy on the outside. (This will add another texture to the dish.)

2) I then put the beef in a bowl with 5 or 6 gnocchi per portion. By then, I'll have sweated off a little spinach in butter and put that on the top for colour, and shall have sliced some peppers, cured them in a little lime juice and salt to make them limp, and garnished the dish with them.

This is a tasty dish which uses a cheap cut of meat, but is full of flavour and the meat melts in your mouth. I have worked with lamb shanks for a while now, but it wasn't until I was working in Australia 2005, at the Bluestone Restaurant in Melbourne, that I found the best way to serve this dish. In the pub I would normally marinate the lamb shanks for twenty-four hours in red wine first, but this is not a necessity.

serves 4 · if marinated lamb required, this needs to be done the previous day

4 lamb shanks
1 large onion
5 cloves garlic
3 carrots
3 stalks of celery
300 ml (11 fl oz) red wine
1 sprig rosemary

1) Preheat oven to 180°C.
2) Season lamb shanks well. Then in a large hot frying pan, with a little oil, colour the lamb shanks well on all sides (almost overcolour because again once braised they will lose some colour).
3) Place the lamb shanks in a roasting tray with roughly-cut vegetables, red wine and enough water to cover the top of the lamb shanks. At this point, you could drop in a crumbled Oxo cube if you want to add flavour.
4) Place tray in oven for 2½ to 3 hours, or until a knife sinks in easily and meat is tender.
5) Remove lamb shanks. Pass the liquid off and in a saucepan reduce it quickly, adding more wine to the sauce if desired, and reduce to sauce consistency.
6) Turn the sauce off. Place a sprig of rosemary in the pan. Leave for 1 min. and then remove the rosemary.

MASHED POTATO

4 large Desirée (red-skinned) potatoes
55g (2 oz) unsalted butter
20ml (1 tbsp) double cream

5g (1 tsp) Dijon mustard
Salt and pepper

1) Peel potatoes and cut into equal-sized pieces. Put them into a large saucepan and fill with water. Bring to boil, then turn down to simmer.
2) Once potatoes are tender, drain off the water and mash them with the butter and cream until smooth.
3) Stir in Dijon mustard and seasoning.

TO FINISH

On the island I would use seasonal vegetables from Ian Metcalf to finish the dish but the choice is yours. In the picture, I have used baby carrots, fine beans and mangetout.

For a guide to US measures, see pp 169, 171 and 187.

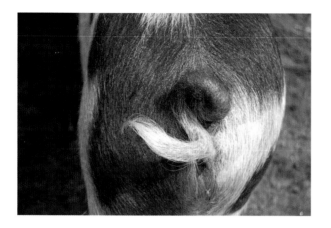 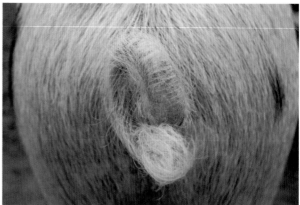

BRAISED PORK BELLY ON RED WINE CABBAGE, WITH SAGE, APPLE AND WALNUT CRUSTED TENDERLOIN, AND CIDER JUS.

This is one of the most popular dishes from the evening menu at the Seven Stones. If you really want to impress your dinner guests, this is the type of dish to do, but plenty of preparation time is needed.

serves 4 · some preparation 24 hours before serving

BRAISED BELLY

I kg (2 lb 4 oz) belly pork
I large carrot
I medium onion
5 cloves garlic
2 sticks celery
12 black peppercorns
2 cans cider

1)   Place belly in a deep roasting tin. Add roughly-chopped vegetables and black peppercorns and pour in the cider. Refrigerate and leave for 24 hours.

2)   Remove from fridge, leaving the vegetables and pork in the roasting tray. Strain off the cider and put to one side. Pour water into the roasting tray to cover the pork.

3) Cover tray with tin foil, place in preheated oven at 160°C and cook out for 3–4 hours, or until a knife passes through the belly with ease.

4) Once cooked, remove belly from liquor and vegetables, then either leave it to cool or press between two trays and leave to cool. The latter will give it better shape on the plate.

5) Pass the liquid through a fine sieve. Retain the cooking liquor for the sauce (see overleaf, p. 156). When you are about to serve, in a hot frying pan colour the belly on all sides, then place on a baking tray and put in hot oven until everything else is ready.

RED WINE CABBAGE

1 head red cabbage
250ml (8½ fl oz) red wine
200ml (6½ fl oz) veal stock (or Bisto!)

1) In a heavy-bottomed saucepan, heat up a small amount of oil. Once hot, add cabbage, season and cook until wilted.

2) Add red wine and reduce down by two thirds.

3) Turn down to a simmer, add the stock and cook out until tender. If juices become too thick before cabbage is cooked add a little water.

SAGE, APPLE AND WALNUT CRUSTED TENDERLOIN

1 large pork tenderloin
2 Granny Smith apples
30g (1 oz) walnuts
15g (½ oz) fresh sage
30g (1 oz) butter
10ml (½ tbsp) cider vinegar

1) In a food processor, blend apple, walnuts, sage, butter and vinegar until smooth.

2) In a hot pan, colour the tenderloin on all sides, then place in preheated oven at 180°C for 6 or 7 mins. Remove and leave to rest for 3 min.

3) Brush the top of the tenderloin liberally with apple and walnut mix, then place under grill until desired colour is achieved. Slice to serve.

CIDER JUS

For the sauce, take the original 2 tins of cider from marinating of the belly (p. 154 instruction 2), reduce by three quarters, then add the passed pork belly liquid (p. 155 note 5) and the braising liquor. Reduce down to sauce consistency. Turn off the heat; add a fresh sprig of sage for 1 min., then remove. Check sauce for seasoning.

TO FINISH

As you can see from the picture I have placed the tenderloin on mashed potato (see lamb shank recipe, p. 152) and the belly on the red cabbage.
I have used wild mushrooms and spinach around the plate to garnish.

Celebration Desserts from the Seven Stones

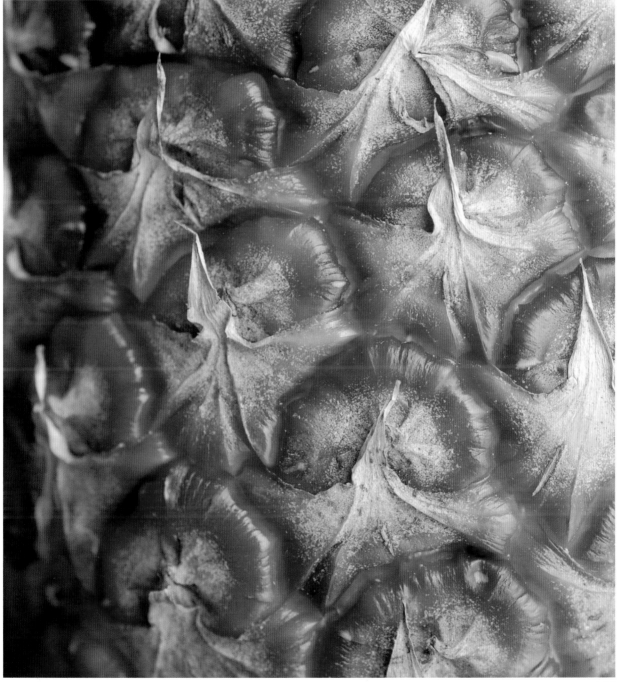

This is a regular on the Seven Stones dessert menu. I first did this dish 'down under' in New Zealand. I had never used candied ginger in cooking before, but now I use it in desserts like this one and even in soups (see p. 92)!

serves 6–8

TOPPING

100g (3½ oz) demerara sugar
6 rounds fresh pineapple

1) Remove the skin and core of the pineapple and cut into rounds about 1cm thick.
2) Dissolve the demerara sugar in 100 ml (3½ fl oz) water and bring it to the boil. Turn down to a simmer, add the pineapple rings, and cook out for 5 min. until the pineapple is soft and tender.
3) Remove pineapple from pan, place on tray and leave to cool. Retain the sugar–water mix for later to decorate the plate.

SPONGE MIX

300g (10½ oz) butter
300g (10½ oz) sugar
5 large eggs
250g (9 oz) self-raising flour
2 tsp baking powder
50g (1¾ oz) ground almonds
75g (2¾ oz) candied ginger

1) Cream the butter and sugar together in a mixing bowl. Add the eggs. The mix may appear to become split at this point, but keep beating it. It will come back. Now add first the flour and then the almonds and the ginger.
2) Line a 15 cm (6-in) baking tin with greaseproof paper, and place the pineapple rings at the bottom of the tray evenly.
3) Put the sponge mix on top and place in pre-heated oven at 180°C for 45 minutes or until springy. Take tray out of oven and leave to cool.
4) Cut into portions of the desired size.

COFFEE CREAM SAUCE

100ml (3½ fl oz) double cream
2 tbsp instant coffee
1 scraped vanilla pod
1 shot of kahlua/coffee liquor (optional)
Black pepper

1) Put all the ingredients except the black pepper into a small saucepan. Bring it to the boil and then turn down and reduce the sauce until a thick consistency is achieved.

2) Remove from the heat and with a pepper mill give a few grinds and stir in. This will warm the sauce. Taste, and add more if desired.

TO FINISH

1) In the picture I have done zigzag lines with the coffee sauce, placed the pudding in the middle, and drizzled the syrup from the pineapple topping around the outside. I've also added a scoop of St Agnes vanilla ice cream.

ROASTED FIGS ON A SHORTCAKE BISCUIT WITH BRANDY SNAP BASKET AND ICE CREAM

Homegrown fresh figs have a very short season; August and September are the months to find them locally. People either love or hate them. I have to say I'm a lover, but if they don't take your fancy, use the same method as below but use plums instead.

Any remaining shortbreads can be covered with melted dark chocolate and served with a coffee or liqueur after dessert, delicious! The brandy snap basket looks complicated but is actually quite easy.

serves 4

ROASTED FIGS

8 ripe figs
200g (7 oz) caster sugar
A few twists of freshly ground black pepper

1) Take a small roasting tin. Cover with the sugar, sit the figs on top, grind black pepper on the top of them, and then place tray in a 180°C preheated oven for 35–40 min., until figs are soft.
2) Once figs are cooked, remove the tray from the oven. Take the cooked figs off, then scrape the remaining juice and sugar into a small saucepan.
3) Reduce this liquor down until a thick syrup is achieved. Retain this for garnishing the dish.

SHORTCAKE BISCUIT

175g (6 oz) self-raising flour, sifted
60g (2 oz) caster sugar
100g (3½ oz) butter (we use salted)

1) Mix or whisk the butter and sugar until light and creamy.
2) Gradually mix in the sifted flour. You will have to get your hands in at this stage, until a silky moist pastry is achieved. Without delay, roll the pastry on a floured table to approximately 5 mm (¼ in) thick and cut into rounds 8–10 cm (3–4 in) across for the finished dessert to sit on top.
3) Bake at 160°C for 8–10 min., or until a light golden brown.

BRANDY SNAP BASKET

110g (4 oz) plain flour
1 tsp ground ginger
50g (2 oz) butter
75g (3 oz) light brown sugar
50g (2 oz) golden syrup

1) Preheat the oven to 180°C. In a mixing bowl, add the flour and ginger.
2) Now in a saucepan mix the butter, sugar and syrup and warm them until all are melted and mixed. Mix into the flour and beat in the syrup until all is combined, then leave to cool.
3) Make small balls of the mixture, either rolling in your hand or using a teaspoon as a rough guide to shape. Space balls well as the mix will melt and spread. Place the tray in the oven for 10–12 min. or until the mix is a golden caramel colour. Leave to cool for 30 sec.
4) You can either cut the brandy snaps into discs with a cutter or while they are still warm press them round the outside of an egg cup to form shape.
5) Leave them to cool. In the picture, I have also used a syrup to add a sharp flavour to the dish—for ease, use syrup out of a stem ginger jar. I have also used St Agnes pistachio ice cream, which accompanies this dish very well.

"**R**unning the Seven Stones kitchen this last season, I have taken on many more responsibilities than before. Ordering on the Scillies can be very difficult because the cargo ship, the Gry Maritha, only sails from Penzance three nights a week (it can be less if bad weather prevails). Occasionally, a box or two full of my requested produce goes astray ... normally to be found at one of the other island businesses! This is why my orders have to be placed a day early.

"All in all, local produce is both more reliable and better. As tripper boats run daily among the islands, I am able to get fresh produce from all over Scilly. For example, local fisherman Martin Bond calls me the morning the fish is landed to see what of his catch I would like; the fish is then put on a tripper boat the same day. That way I get excellent quality fresh local fish on a daily basis. As for vegetables and herbs, they come from Ian Metcalf on St Martin's itself. I get what I need every day for my kitchen, but if I run out you'll see me running down to the garden and picking more!

"At the Seven Stones we've catered for functions with up to a hundred and fifty people. One such was islanders Ryan and Lois Allsop's wedding, where the band Roadrunner played in the marquee. Island versatility is never far away: the marquee would later become great for the campers who lost their tents in the strong winds which hit the island in Whitsun week! We set up a garden heater and put on a barbeque for the soaked campers. Later, the marquee would fall to a similar fate when strong winds from the south battered the islands. They damaged its roof beyond repair, and wind- and rain-sodden staff picked up the pieces early next morning.

"Developing the menu through the season has inevitably involved a learning curve, and we've offered both classic pub meals and gastro pub dishes. In the school summer holidays, we would also offer an early dinner menu, providing balanced meals for the kids.

"I'm looking forward to my next season, where I can land with my feet running. The kitchen is now organised and equipped; I have a three-strong brigade with Kris and Lydia coming back. We've all got new ideas and improvements lined up. Experience has been telling me for a while now that like islanders over the centuries, we've just got to push ourselves, all the way."

PAULIE WEBSDALE

Traditional Pastries and the Bakery's own Lemonade

This simplest of recipes was sent to me by my sister Marie from her home in Grenoble in the south of France.

It uses the sweetened, egg-including pastry, pâte à foncer, introduced on page 122, and is fantastic either as a dessert tart cut into slices, or as individual teatime treats (shown).

There is another photo on page 163.

Marie Robichon

makes one large 30 cm (12-in) tart or 24 small tarts

PÂTE À FONCER

Use the recipe given on p. 122.

LEMON FILLING

300g (10½ oz) ground almonds
100g (3½ oz) icing sugar
150g (5 oz) caster sugar
Zest and juice of 2 lemons
125g (4½ oz) melted butter
4 eggs
Apricot jam to glaze
   (if required for show)

1) Make the pastry according to the recipe on page 122. Chill it in the fridge while you are making the filling.
2) For the filling, mix the ground almonds with the two types of sugar. Whisk the eggs separately and add to the almonds and sugars. Next, add the melted butter and lemon zest and juice to this, until a smooth consistency is arrived at. We sometimes add the sievings from our lemonade (see p. 174) to make this really lush.
3) Roll out the pastry thinly.
4) If making into one large tart, remember to overlap the pastry slightly and trim after to give a good edge.
5) For individual tarts, cut into 10 cm (4-in) rounds. Push these round discs into the cups of a muffin tray.
6) Fill the pastry cups or 30 cm (12-in) tart tin with the lemon mixture.
7) Bake at 200°C until golden, approx. 20 min. When cooled a little, glaze with melted apricot jam.

For a guide to US measures, see pp 169 and 171 or 187.

There are many Tarte Tatin recipes to be found in books, some of which require the alchemy of bubbling caramel on hobs. This recipe is my sister Marie's, from Grenoble in France, and is the quickest of creations. This upside-down caramelised apple tart is fantastic served hot, but we normally allow it to cool and set before eating with cream, clotted cream, or fantastic St Agnes ices. It also works wonderfully with pears cut into halves and laid round-side down—great with a hint of fresh mint. For the sweet pastry follow the simple recipe on page 111.

makes one 30 cm (12-in) tart

PASTRY

400g (14 oz) flour
200g (7 oz) margarine or butter
100g (3½ oz) sugar
Water to bind

APPLE MIX

Two large cooking apples
Golden brown sugar, to taste and depending on the apples used
Dark sugar, as above
Cinnamon and a large knob of butter

Making Tarte Tatin on a Bakery course

1) Make the pastry (see p. 111 if you do not already have some prepared).
2) Peel and core the apples and cut into segments about 1 cm thick.
3) Take a 30 cm (12-in) metal pizza pan and cover to a depth of about 5 mm (¼-in) with a combination of the sugars. Arrange the apples in a ring all in one direction around the outside. Perhaps take the opposite direction with the next ring, and so on until you have covered the pan. Add the butter on top in lumps. Sprinkle a generous amount of cinnamon over the apples.
4) Roll out your sweet pastry and carefully cover the apples, leaving a small overlap to retain the melted sugars.
5) Glaze with beaten egg and bake for 25 min. at 200–220°C on a baking tray.
6) Remove from the oven and with gloves and great care invert the pan onto another pizza pan. Tap to free any apples which may stick and slowly prise the top pan away, to reveal your beautiful tart.

TREACLE TART

It's not often we have bread left over during the season. None sadly makes it to my empty bread bin at home!—for if we have any, nothing is wasted and the loaves, trimmed of their crusts, are turned into breadcrumbs to make the most delicious, heavy treacle tarts—not to be consumed before a swim! The added zing is provided by the sievings from our lemonade (see p. 174) or the zest and juices from lemons. It's irresistible when served with St Agnes clotted or ice cream.

for one 30 cm (12-in) treacle tart

FILLING

200g (7 oz) cake margarine
500ml (1.1 pints) golden syrup
Zest and juice of one lemon (or lemonade sievings)
One loaf, crust discarded (our pigs are happy!) and turned into breadcrumbs

PASTRY

400g (14 oz) white flour (we use strong white, but plain flour is good)
200g (7 oz) cake margarine, or butter for a shorter pastry
100g (3½ oz) caster sugar
1 egg yolk (optional)

1) In effect, this is a 4:2:1 sweet pastry (see page 111). Use water (approximately 200 ml, just under ½ pint) to bind the ingredients into a soft pastry, but maybe add a free-range egg yolk to make it richer. Chill it in the fridge to relax.

2) Meanwhile, heat the margarine for the filling in a pan on the hob. Add the golden syrup and lemon juice or zest; keep stirring so that it doesn't catch.

3) When loose and hot, add the breadcrumbs.

4) Roll the chilled pastry into an oiled flan dish (overlapping the side of the dish, to be later trimmed when cooked and cooled, for that professional look).

5) Fill with the breadcrumb/syrup mixture. There is no need to prebake the pastry.

6) Scatter a sprinkling of sliced almonds on the top for taste and decoration.
7) Bake at 200°C for 20–25 min., or until golden brown. And blow up the armbands if you're swimming later, you'll need all the help you can get!

US MEASURES

Scilly may be one of the nearest parts of the UK to the USA but it's still very conscious of its British weights and measures and of the metric ones which—whether or not we Brits like them!—are here to stay. For the benefit of North American readers of this book, conversion tables based on cups, and Celsius to Fahrenheit scales, are given on page 187. American readers should beware measures in pints. The traditional imperial pint (everyone in the UK knows what a pint of beer and a pint of milk look like!) is a bigger measure than the US pint (1 US pint=0.83 imperial pints). The American cup measure is exactly half a US pint, but it's only just over 0.4 imperial pints. Unfortunately, ounces (oz) to cups is no easier: 8 oz (250g) = 1 cup is standard, but it varies according to the ingredient being measured. Thus 1 cup of flour is 140g (4½ oz), of sugar 200g (7 oz), of grated cheese 100g (3½ oz). For more, see over, p. 171.

The result of humanity's crossbreeding seeds is to create flours which have such a high gluten content that they can have damaging effect on some people's digestive systems. Consequently we are being asked more and more for gluten-free products.

Many years ago Natalie worked at the bakery. She had not only a sweet tooth but also a problem with eating some flours. Therefore we created this gluten-free dish for her to enjoy and the many returning visitors who know we always offer one type of gluten-free cake each day.

In the recipe, we use bicarbonate of soda and cream of tartar because most commercial premixed baking powders contain flour. For the fruit, we use at different times plums, nectarines, peaches, banana and pineapple.

makes one 30 cm (12-in) cake

300g (10½ oz) margarine
300g (10½ oz) caster and/or brown sugar,
   and a bit more to cover the flan dish
4 eggs
300g (10½ oz) gluten-free flour
1 tsp cream of tartar
1 tsp bicarbonate of soda
50g (1¾ oz) ground almonds
1 tbsp almond flavouring
Enough fruit, as above, to cover the bottom of a 30 cm (12-in) flan dish

1) Line a deep flan dish of the suggested size with silicon paper. Cover this with two handfuls of the sugars.

2) In a food processor, whiz the sugar and the margarine together. Add the four eggs and whiz some more. Next, add the flours with the raising agents, and also at this stage add the ground almonds and almond flavouring. Blend all of this mix into a smooth consistency.

3) Arrange your chosen fruit on top of the sugar in the flan dish. Carefully spread the sponge mix evenly on top of the fruit. Cover with some silicon paper to prevent catching, and bake at 200°C for approximately 25 min.

4) A cleanly withdrawn skewer indicates that the sponge is thoroughly cooked. Free the edge of the cooked sponge from the side of the dish with a sharp

knife. Wearing oven gloves, place another, same-sized, flan dish on top. Invert.

5) Carefully remove the silicon paper which was under the fruit. Stand back and admire your work with its surprising finish.

US MEASURES (see also pp. 169 and 187)

THE VARIABLE WEIGHT EQUIVALENTS OF CUP MEASURES

1 cup flour = 140g
1 cup sugar = 200g
1 cup icing sugar = 125g
1 cup rice = 200g
1 cup frozen peas = 125g
1 cup fresh breadcrumbs = 70g
1 cup grated cheese - 100g
1 cup raisins or sultanas = 150g
1 cup honey/syrup = 300g

Although a pie not a tart, this obviously belongs here. When the frenetic activity of August is over, we have a happy time foraging for the bursting blackberries swelled by September's warm sun and coinciding with the ripening of Audrey's Bramley apple trees. This is an opportunity not to be missed for that fantastic and most traditional Island dessert.

The pastry used is Pâte à Foncer *(p. 122), to give a nice shortness. St Agnes Clotted Cream or Ice Cream is delicious with this celebration of Island bounty.*

makes one 30cm (12-in) pie

Pastry as on p. 122, *Pâte à Foncer,* in a double quantity
7–8 large Bramley apples
60g (2½ oz) butter (we use salted)
3 tbsps of soft brown sugar
A handful of sultanas
1 teaspoon of cinnamon, or ½ grated nutmeg
100 ml (3½ fl oz) water

1) Make the pastry, doubling the amount on page 122 as this pie also has a lid. Cling-wrap and refrigerate while you begin the filling.

2) Peel, core and cut the apples into small chunks.

3) Melt the butter in a heavy-based pan and sauté the apples. Add the sugar and keep heating.

4) Next add the cinnamon, water and sultanas and gently bubble, stirring occasionally to break down the apples into a texture resembling lumpy babyfood. Remove from the heat.

5) On a floured table, roll out half of the pastry to fit and overlap a greased or oiled flan dish.

6) Pour in the apple mixture, then dot the surface of the apples with a good handful of plump blackberries (sampling one or two, of course)!

7) Paint the edge of the overlapped pastry with beaten egg or milk to aid sticking the lid on.

8) Roll out the other half of the pastry on a floured table again. We roll, cut and decorate the pastry lid at this stage with a pastry lattice cutter; a sharp knife will do the same job.

9) Roll this second lot of pastry around your pin and carefully cover the filled pie with some overlap. Trim with scissors close to the flan dish.

10) Squeeze the two pastries together to form a seal. We then crimp the two pastries together by holding thumb and forefinger of our left hand on top of the pastry about 25 mm (1 in) apart. With the forefinger of the right hand we drag the pastry inwards from the edge of the dish, between thumb and forefinger. The dragged pastry is then squeezed between the thumb and forefinger of the left hand to seal and form an attractive crimp, which will also keep the cooked pie together when served.

11) Glaze with beaten egg to brown and scatter with caster or brown sugar as preferred.

12) Bake at 200°C for 22–25 min.

For a guide to US measures, see pp 169, 171 and 187.

CORNISH LEMONADE

Before we move on to the teatime recipes, time for a drink! We chose many years ago not to provide coffees and teas as we do today in the Bakery but to offer a distinctly different drink for those hot and languid summer days on St Martin's. I found an old Cornish recipe for lemonade in Pamela Pascoe's COUSIN JENNIE'S COOKBOOK *which, with some small changes, would produce a delicious drink.*

Today, our lemonade has gathered some notoriety—with people making the pilgrimage to the bakery on recommendation to try this fantastic instant energy-hit. It is the easiest of recipes and makes an absolutely delicious thirst-quenching drink.
It will last for a couple of weeks in concentrated form in the fridge, or can be frozen in small amounts for later use. However, remember to stir well each time you dilute it.

makes 15 pints

10 lemons and 5 oranges
30g (1 oz) citric acid
30g (1 oz) tartaric acid
   (these acids can be bought from home-brew shops, Boots, etc.)
1.75kg (4 lbs) soft brown sugar
   (if a portion of this is dark muscovado sugar, say about 200g (7 oz), it
   gives an attractive extra deepness)
2½ litres (4 pints) water, more to dilute before serving

1)   Zest all of the lemons and oranges into a large saucepan, taking care not to get too much white pith in with it, or it will taste bitter.

2)   Next, squeeze all of the lemons and oranges onto the gratings. To this, add the sugar, the initial water, and both of the acids.

3)   Gradually heat until the sugar is dissolved, stirring occasionally. Set aside to cool.

4)   When cool, sieve and dilute one part lemon to three parts water, and serve chilled! The sievings can be used to enhance treacle tart or lemon tarts (see pp. 168, 164).

THE ISLAND INGREDIENT

Teatime and Coffeetime Treats

Turkish by invention, not French as many people assume, croissants are not difficult to make, but have many stages of production, which renders them a labour of love. The recipe below can be halved and the cooked croissant can be clingwrapped and frozen for later use very successfully. We use this croissant dough recipe to create our Pains au Raisin *and Danish pastries so it is a versatile dough allowing us many alternatives from one method of production.*

approx. 30 croissants or 15 croissants and 15 *pains au raisin*
requires advance preparation, possibly the day before

POOLISH

60g (2 oz) fresh yeast
2 eggs
1 tsp sugar
700 ml (1½ pints) milk and water, mixed 50:50
A large handful of flour

MIX

1 kg (2 lb 4 oz) strong flour
500g (1 lb 2 oz) salted butter
1 tbsp salt
8 tbsp caster sugar

1) Dissolve the yeast with the milk/water and whisk in the eggs, the handful of flour and a teaspoon of sugar to start the yeast working. Set aside. This mixture will rise actively, after about an hour or so in a warm kitchen.

2) Mix the flour with the caster sugar and salt and add the enriched poolish starter. Work into a smooth dough.

3) Set aside, covered, to be allowed to approximately double in size.

4) Next roll out into a large rectangle and mark into thirds with your finger., tracing a gentle line. Split the butter into three more or less equal amounts,

and dot one of the lumps over the middle and the right hand thirds of the dough. Fold the butterless left-hand third of the dough over the middle third and the right-hand third on top of this. Leave for 5 min. to relax the gluten.

5) Turn the dough 90° anticlockwise. Roll out into a rectangle again and repeat the dotting of butter onto the middle and right-hand thirds, folding as before.

6) Repeat once more after a similar break, using up the last block of butter. Leave the dough now, covered with cling film, and in the fridge, for at least an hour, to allow the yeast to begin to work on the fats introduced to the dough. We leave the buttered dough overnight in the fridge for the remaining rolling and folding to be done early the following morning to have the croissant ready for breakfast.

7) Take from the fridge and repeat the rolling and folding three more times without adding any more butter. This is to increase the layers of lamination of the final croissant.

8) You now have the basic dough which we use for Danish pastries, *pains au raisin*, chocolate and nut whirls, peach and cherry whirls, indeed anything that takes your fancy!

9) Finally, for croissants, roll out the risen dough into a rectangle, to a depth of approximately 1 cm (½ in). It will deflate as you roll. Cut the rectangle into triangles approximately 120 mm (4–5 in.) and roll away, the base side nearest to you keeping the point underneath so it will not uncurl itself when proving or cooking. Glaze with egg and leave to prove in a warm place or an oven (not turned on!) with a bowl of steaming water inside.

10) When dough is nicely fluffed up, bake for 18 min. at 200°C.

The pains au raisin *and Danish pastries we make at the bakery are made of croissant dough (see previous), with various additions and manipulations.*

makes 15, using half the quantity of croissant dough from the previous, as suggested

CRÈME PATISSIÈRE

> 600 ml (1 pint) milk
> 200g (7 oz) caster sugar
> 2 free-range eggs
> 600 ml (1 pint) single/double cream
> 100g (3½ oz) custard powder
>   with
> 1 can of peach slices
> 3 handfuls of raisins
> A splash of almond flavouring (optional)

The Bakery's in sight—and so are our pains au raisin!

1) Warm the milk and cream in a heavy-based saucepan. Add the sugar and heat a little more until it is dissolved, also the almond essence, if using. Remove from the hob. Mix the eggs with the custard powder and whisk into the warmed milk. Put this back on the hob and continue to heat, constantly stirring and even whisking until the mixture thickens considerably.

2) Remove from the stove and pour onto a tray that will fit in the refrigerator. Cover with cling film while still hot to prevent a skin forming, and refrigerate to further set the *crème*.

3) Taking the croissant dough at stage 8 of the previous recipe, roll it out into a rectangle and liberally spread the cooled set *crème* all over. Lavishly spread the raisins all over the *crème*, distribute the peach slices evenly over them, and then roll up to form a spiral tube like a Swiss roll.

4) Cut slices off this, 2 cm (¾-in) thick. Place them on a well-greased baking tray, covered with a light damp cloth or loosely-placed cling film. As you set them out, make sure that the 'key', which is the tail end of the roll, is tucked underneath each *pain au raisin* to stop the spiral from unravelling when cooked. Glaze with beaten egg, and allow them to rest and rise for 20 min.

5) Place in a reasonably high oven, 200–220°C, and bake for 18–20 min.

6) A glaze of sugar, lemon juice and milk can be painted on while still hot to give a lovely glossy sheen.

HOT CROSS BUNS

Up to Easter and beyond we make approximately 1,200 hot cross buns! Each one is rolled by hand and with the crosses, made of flour mixed with water, piped onto trays bulging with the fruit-studded buns. We pipe the trays, 24 to each tray, in vertical and then horizontal sweeps. My first attempt at piping the buns individually ended up in mini swastikas, not very seasonal at all!

for about 12 buns

POOLISH STARTER

30g (1 oz) fresh yeast
1 tsp sugar
300 ml (½ pint) milk and 300 ml (½ pint) water
1 large handful of white flour
1 egg

THE FLOUR MIX

1 kg (2 lbs 4oz) flour (we use ordinary organic strong white)
1 tsp of salt
150g (4½ oz) caster sugar, or brown if you prefer
200g (7 oz) currants
100g (3½ oz) sultanas
50g (1¾ oz) mixed peel
2 free-range eggs
125g (4½ oz) melted butter
1 tbsp mixed spice
1 tsp each nutmeg and cinnamon

DECORATION AND GLAZE

For the crosses:
500g (1 lb 2 oz) flour with water,
    to a smooth paste that can be piped adequately
For the glaze:
1 beaten egg
50ml (3 tbsp) milk
A tablespoon of caster sugar

1) Whisk all the poolish ingredients together and leave for at least an hour to begin to create a yeast-rich colony.

2) Add the working poolish to the dry ingredients, incorporating the melted butter at this stage. If the dough is still a little dry, some additional milk can be added to make smooth silky dough and it will help keep the finished buns soft, as any fat of animal origin added to any dough will render the finished crumb light in texture.

3) Leave to prove, until the dough is at least 50% larger than the original size.

4) Knead and knock back again, leaving for a further half hour.

5) Roll out the dough into a long sausage on the table, 6–7 cm (2½ in) in diameter. Cut the roll into pieces of dough roughly this size across.

6) With a firm downward pressure, roll the pieces of dough into firm rounds which rise to fill the palm of your hand. Don't over-roll or they will become sticky in your hand; don't be worried about the fruit migrating to the outside of each roll, either. This fruit can be picked off and incorporated in the next rolls. Leave to prove again until they have grown in size by 50%.

7) Now pipe on the flour/water mixture to make the crosses.

8) Bake for 20 min. at 200–220°C. While still warm, paint with a non sticky-glaze made of the ingredients opposite. Our first *sticky* glaze delivery to Tresco stores ended up in a mass of 150 welded buns which arrived as one solid block. It wasn't repeated!

In the West Country, no holiday is complete without at least one fantastic cream tea. With local organic strawberries and jam at our disposal, the exceptional St Agnes clotted cream and butter, and our handmade scones, we are well able to provide a taste of summer and satisfy those indulgent urges! We make both plain scones and fruit scones, with currants, raisin and mixed peel. Here is the recipe for plain scones; add fruit as you feel fit.

makes 20

900g (2 lb) organic self-raising flour
100g (3½ oz) caster sugar
250g (9 oz) soft butter (we use salted)
4 free-range eggs plus 1 extra for glaze
2 tsp baking powder (no more, or you will not achieve a good rise)
Milk to bind (we also add some soured milk for extra flavour and rise)

1)   Simply mix the above ingredients in a kitchen food mixer on slow speed with paddle attachment, or by hand in a bowl to achieve a smooth silky dough.

2)   Roll out on a floured table to a depth of about 4 cm (1½ in) and cut with a plain or fluted round scone cutter. Glaze with beaten egg and bake for 12–15 min. at 200–220°C. Cool on a wire rack before attempting to cut and devour.

DATE SLICE

This is my favourite tray bake in the Bakery. It's delicious with a coffee in the early hours, to prepare myself for that inevitable morning rush as the campers and visitors wake up and the boats from other islands begin to land on St Martin's quays. It is basically a simple crumble recipe with a lush date filling, incredibly easy to make and very long-lasting.
If you have a kitchen aid (mixer) with a paddle to mix, all well and good. If not, the crumble can be mixed by hand in a large bowl. We use new washing-up bowls for this on our Holiday Baking Courses.

makes 30

THE BASE AND TOPPING

620g (1¼ lb) self-raising flour
620g (1¼ lb) caster sugar
620g (1¼ lb) rolled oats
620g (1¼ lb) cake margarine

THE DATE FILLING

800g (1¾ lb) chopped dates (ours come rolled in rice flour)
Water to just cover the dates
½ tbsp vanilla essence

1) Mix the base/topping mixture to a breadcrumb consistency.
2) Take half and roll out approximately 5 mm (¼ in) thick with a rolling pin onto a silicon-papered tray.
3) Add the water and vanilla essence to the dates and warm on a hob stirring constantly to prevent burning. A babyfood consistency is required.
4) Spread the date mixture with a spatula over the rolled base.
5) Crumble the other half of the flour/oat/sugar/margarine mixture on top of the dates.
6) Strew with some caster or golden brown sugar to achieve a crisp crunchiness on the finished slices.
7) Bake for 20–25 min. at 200–220°C. Leave to cool before cutting. Put the coffee on!

LISA'S CARAMEL SLICE (MILLIONNAIRES' SHORTBREAD)

A chocolate and caramel temptation that is impossible to resist. More energy is spent refilling the display trays than with any other cake we sell. We alternate the decoration between sprinkling the melted chocolate topping with white or dark chocolate chips, but if we have more time we like to pour lines of melted white chocolate on top of the liquid dark chocolate and drag with the back of a knife in alternate directions to create a feather-type pattern which is suitably seductive.

makes 30. Don't worry, they won't hang around!

For the base:
750g (1 lb 10 oz) self-raising flour
450g (1 lb) cake margarine or butter
200g (7 oz) caster sugar

For the caramel topping:
200g (7 oz) cake margarine or butter
150g (5 oz) golden syrup
200g (7 oz) soft brown sugar
600g (1 lb 5 oz) condensed milk
Good dark melting chocolate

1) In a kitchen mixer, if you have one (if not, using a mixing bowl and hands), combine all the materials for the base into a soft dough. Roll or press this dough out onto a silicon-papered oven tray. Prick all over with a fork.

2) Bake at 200°C for 12–15 min., or until golden brown.

3) While the base is cooking, melt the fat for the topping in a heavy-based pan. Add the golden syrup and continue to stir on the stove. Next add the brown sugar and finally pour in the condensed milk.

4) Continue to stir with a long-handled wooden spoon on a high heat, until the caramel begins to change to a darker colour and thicken. Do not stop stirring at any point or the caramel will burn on the bottom of the pan.

5) Don't worry if you find some dark flecks in the mixture. Keep stirring until the mixture comes to boiling point. This temperature must be achieved to enable the caramel to set later. Be careful not to get splashed with the hot sticky mixture.

6) Remove from the heat, but continue to stir for a minute or so to prevent burning.
7) Pour the liquid caramel on your golden-baked base. Put aside to cool and start to set.
8) Melt some good cocoa-rich melting chocolate in a double boiler if you have one. If not, a large pan of moderately hot water with a smaller pan immersed into it and the chocolate in the smaller pan will do.
9) Spread the melted chocolate on top of the cooled and set caramel. and decorate however you wish: chocolate pips, dragged white chocolate or mixed nuts. To prevent the topping from cracking, cut the slices when the chocolate has just cooled and set.
10) Devour with a good cup of coffee (no, not all of them!).

LISA'S SCRUMPTIOUS SLICE

This is another of Lisa Bowery's fantastic recipes which we have used since eight years ago Lisa helped in the conversion of this abandoned barn into St Martin's Bakery. She spent her days sanding and painting and her evenings brushing up on my baking skills, persuaded by the results of my teachings and a glass of wine to help swallow my occasional burnt offerings!

The recipe uses broken digestive biscuits, but any broken biscuits or cake past its best can be used up.

makes 12 good slices

350g (12 oz) digestive/broken biscuits
170g (6 oz) margarine or butter
60g (2 oz) caster sugar
120g (4 oz) golden syrup
4 tbsp cocoa powder
120g (4 oz) mixed chopped nuts
120g (4 oz) glace cherries
120g (4 oz) raisins
240g (8 oz) dark organic melting chocolate

1) Crumb the digestive/broken biscuits, either in a food processor or by beating the biscuits in a freezer bag with a rolling pin. Don't be too worried about leaving the biscuits too finely broken.

2) Melt the margarine in a heavy pan; add the sugar and syrup and continue to heat.

3) Thoroughly mix in the cocoa powder, or if you have no cocoa powder melt 120g (4 oz) of organic dark chocolate separately in a double boiler and add.

4) Next, add the mixed chopped nuts, and half the glacé cherries and half the raisins. Roll or press onto a baking tray and bake at 180°C for 10 min.

5) For the topping, melt the organic dark chocolate in a double boiler, or improvise with two pans (see previous recipe, step 8). Spread the melted chocolate on top of the still warm base.

6) Scatter over the remaining cherries and nuts.

7) Tap the whole tray to fix the cherries and nuts in place.

8) Set aside to cool, cut into slices before the chocolate sets too hard and refrigerate.

THE ISLAND INGREDIENT

US MEASURES (see the note on cups, p. 171, and the general note, p. 169)

| 1 US liquid cup | 8 (UK) fl oz | 0.42 imperial pints | 239 ml |

Weight/volume conversion (imperial to cups)

2 oz	.25 cup
4 oz	.5 cup
6 oz	.75 cup
8 oz	1 cup
10 oz	1.25 cups
12 oz	1.5 cups 1
14 oz	1.75 cups
16 oz (1 lb)	2 cups
24 oz (1 lb 8 oz)	3cups
32 oz (2 lb)	4 cups

(grams and kilos to cups)

100g	.44 cup
250g	1.1 cups
500g	2.2 cups
1 kg	4.4 cups

Oven Temperatures

110°C (gas 1)	230°F
175°C (gas 4)	347°F
200°C (gas 6)	392°F
220°C (gas 8)	428°F

BASIC SPONGE MIX AND CHOCOLATE COFFEE FILLING

We have many holiday visitors enjoying a birthday here and are constantly asked to provide celebration cakes for these occasions. Here is our basic sponge mix, either plain or chocolate. If we are making the chocolate one we usually cover the sponge cake with more melted chocolate, into which we set local organic strawberries. It then becomes a celebration cake to be savoured.

makes one 20 cm (8-in) cake

225g (8 oz) cake margarine
225g (8 oz) caster sugar
275g (10 oz) organic self-raising flour
2 level tsp baking powder
   (any more and your cake will deflate after cooking)
4 free-range eggs
4 tbsp milk
3 tbsp cocoa powder if making a chocolate sponge

1)   Whiz all of these ingredients in a kitchen food processor.
2)   Line a 20 cm (8-in.) cake tin with silicon paper and fill with the sponge mix.
3)   Cover and bake at 180°C for about 35 min. A cleanly-withdrawn skewer indicates the cake is cooked.

CHOCOLATE COFFEE CREAM FILLING

1 heaped tsp instant coffee
60g (2 oz) caster sugar
125g (4½ oz) butter
1 free-range egg yolk
3 tbsp grated dark organic chocolate

1)   To three tablespoons of cold water add the teaspoon of instant coffee and the sugar. Mix well, then heat on the hob until it is bubbling thickly.
2)   Remove from the heat. Whisk in one free-range egg yolk and the grated melted, dark organic chocolate to obtain a frothy mixture.
3)   Next whisk in the butter until a smooth consistency is arrived at. Chill in the fridge for later spreading onto the cooled, cut-in-half sponge.

Index to Place Names, People and Things of Interest

Food Index

Note: dishes suitable for vegetarians are shown in green. For US measures, see pp 169 and 171 or 187